The Horse That Won't Go Away

Clever Hans, Facilitated Communication, and the Need for Clear Thinking

Thomas E. Heinzen
William Paterson University

Scott O. Lilienfeld
Emory University

Susan A. Nolan
Seton Hall University

WORTH
PUBLISHERS

A Macmillan Education Imprint
New York

Publisher: Rachel Losh
Senior Acquisitions Editor: Daniel DeBonis
Development Editor: Elsa Peterson
Editorial Assistant: Katie Pachnos
Senior Marketing Manager: Lindsay Johnson
Marketing Assistant: Allison Greco
Director of Editing, Design, and Media Production: Tracey Kuehn
Managing Editor: Lisa Kinne
Production Editor: Janice Stangel
Production Manager: Sarah Segal
Photo Editor: Richard Fox
Art Director: Diana Blume
Interior and Cover Designer: Kevin Kall
Art Manager: Matthew McAdams
Illustrations: Lachina
Composition: Linda Harms
Printing and Binding: RR Donnelley

Library of Congress Preassigned Control Number: 2014956522
ISBN-10: 1-4641-4574-1
ISBN-13: 978-1-4641-4574-2

Printed in the United States of America
First printing

Worth Publishers
41 Madison Avenue
New York, NY 10010
www.worthpublishers.com

For Michael Brown
—Tom Heinzen

To James Randi, tireless and fearless slayer of myths
—Scott Lilienfeld

For Ranko Bojanic
—Susan Nolan

Thomas E. Heinzen is Professor of Psychology at William Paterson University of New Jersey. A graduate of Rockford College, he earned his Ph.D. in social psychology at the State University of New York at Albany. After publishing his first book on frustration and creativity in government, Heinzen worked as a public policy research associate, consulted for the Johns Hopkins Center for Talented Youth, and then began his teaching career. He founded William Paterson University's Psychology Club, established an undergraduate research conference, and has been awarded various teaching honors while continuing to write articles, books, and plays that support the teaching of general psychology and statistics. Heinzen, a fellow of the Eastern Psychological Association, is also the editor of *Many Things to Tell You*, a volume of poetry by elderly writers. His current research involves applying game design to higher education.

Scott O. Lilienfeld is Professor of Psychology at Emory University in Georgia. He received his bachelor's degree from Cornell University and his Ph.D. in psychology (clinical) from the University of Minnesota. Lilienfeld is Associate Editor of the *Journal of Abnormal Psychology*, President of the Society for the Scientific Study of Psychopathy, and past President of the Society for a Science of Clinical Psychology. He has published over 300 articles, chapters, and books on personality and dissociative disorders, psychiatric classification, pseudoscience in psychology, and evidence-based practices in clinical psychology. A Fellow of the Committee for Skeptical Inquiry and a columnist for *Scientific American Mind*, Lilienfeld was a recipient of the David Shakow Award for Outstanding Early Career Contributions to Clinical Psychology and the James McKeen Cattell Award for Distinguished Career Contributions to Applied Psychological Science.

Susan A. Nolan is Professor of Psychology at Seton Hall University in New Jersey. A graduate of the College of the Holy Cross, she earned her Ph.D. in psychology from Northwestern University. Susan researches interpersonal consequences of mental illness and the role of gender in science and technology fields. Her research has been funded by the National Science Foundation. Susan served as a nongovernmental representative from the American Psychological Association (APA) to the United Nations for five years, and is Vice President for Diversity and International Relations of the Society for the Teaching of Psychology. She is the 2014–2015 President of the Eastern Psychological Association (EPA), and is a Fellow of both EPA and APA.

CONTENTS

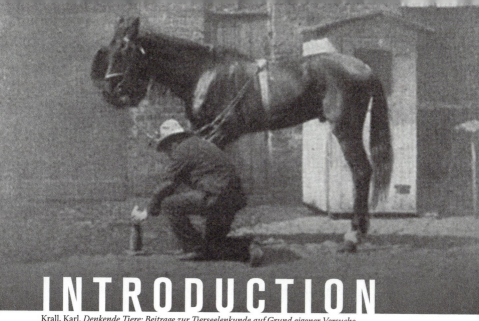

INTRODUCTION

Krall, Karl. *Denkende Tiere: Beitrage zur Tierseelenkunde auf Grund eigener Versuche.*
Leipzig: Engelmann, 1912, p.14.

Why It's Important to Be a Clear Thinker

*The first principle is that you should not fool yourself—and you
are the easiest person to fool.*

Richard P. Feynman

Clear thinking (also called critical thinking) is the hallmark of
psychological science. The two stories you are about to read
demonstrate how clear thinking works and why it is so important. The first is a story about a determined teacher and his belief
that he could teach an ordinary horse to think. The second story is about children and adults with communications difficul-
ties (often attributed to autism) and the dedicated professionals
who try to help them based on their belief in a therapeutic technique called *facilitated communication*. However, both of these
stories are really about all of us and our propensity to believe in

1

things that cannot be true. Both accounts are well documented and there is no disagreement about the historical or scientific facts. As a result, we have the best seats in the house to watch as self-deception creeps into these lives and how clear, critical thinking brought some people back to their senses.

A classic *Sesame Street* skit (check it out on YouTube) featuring Bert and Ernie illustrates why we are so enthusiastic about the possibilities of clear thinking:

Bert approaches Ernie, who has a banana in his ear.

Bert: "Why is that banana still in your ear?"

Ernie: "Listen, Bert, I use this banana to keep the alligators away."

Bert: "Alligators? Ernie, there are no alligators on *Sesame Street.*"

Ernie: "Right! It's doing a good job, isn't it, Bert?"

Not surprisingly, Bert is flabbergasted because (a) it's a safe bet that alligators aren't frightened of bananas; and (b) it's easier to spot someone else's crazy beliefs than to spot our own. Ernie perceived evidence that the banana was working, but Ernie's evidence was what psychologists call an **illusory correlation**—believing in a connection that does not exist.

Such false beliefs are sometimes called **mind bugs,** small misconceptions that cause systematic mental errors.[1] The best way to diminish the negative effects of false beliefs is by practicing clear, critical thinking. The word "critical" is often associated with finding fault, but a **clear, critical thinker** is not someone who readily finds fault with others. In fact, good critical

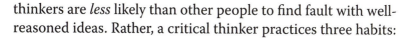

thinkers are *less* likely than other people to find fault with well-reasoned ideas. Rather, a critical thinker practices three habits:

1. healthy skepticism;
2. the humility to admit mistakes; and
3. the courage to think independently in the face of expert and popular opinion.

For example, imagine the four possible outcomes in a matrix that Bert could have used to help Ernie see that the correlation he perceives is an illusion.

ALLIGATORS AND BANANAS	ALLIGATORS NOT PRESENT	ALLIGATORS PRESENT
BANANA IN EAR TO REPEL ALLIGATORS	What Ernie observed in this *Sesame Street* episode	What Ernie might have observed had he tried this in the Everglades
NO BANANA IN EAR TO REPEL ALLIGATORS	What Ernie ignored in all of the other *Sesame Street* episodes where he did *not* have a banana in his ear	What Ernie might have observed had he traveled to the Everglades without a banana

Ernie is only paying attention to the quadrant in the upper left and is ignoring the three other possibilities. Of course, Ernie is a fictional character; surely, intelligent human beings don't think this way—or do they? Let's raise the stakes by considering the preparations made by one of the book's authors (Susan) whenever a hurricane was bearing down on the places where she has lived. Believing that if a wind gust blew out a window, a crisscross pattern of masking tape would keep glass shards from scattering into the home and injuring someone, Susan would routinely tape up her windows. In fact, she thought the tape might even make the windows stronger and less likely to break.

This strategy seemed to work. Each time she played tic-tac-toe on her windows, the glass survived the hurricane intact. Her belief was confirmed because it worked for her and for her neighbors, so she perceived a possibly life-saving correlation between taping the windows and riding out a hurricane safely. But Susan's faith in this preventive act was—unlike her windows—shattered in 2011 when she saw warnings on a news program *against* using tape in this way.

Only then did she conduct a little further research on the National Weather Service (NWS) Web site. There, she learned the NWS warns that taped windows actually *increase* the risk of injury because pieces of broken glass that are taped tend to be larger and can become dangerous projectiles in high winds. Instead, the NWS advises those in the path of a hurricane to protect windows with plywood or storm shutters.[2]

How did Susan come to believe in something that was both wrong and dangerous? She had always noticed the taped windows in the neighborhoods where she lived, all of which remained intact, while ignoring all of the *un*taped windows that also remained intact. Plus, she had been lucky and escaped each hurricane's wrath unscathed. She never experienced unsafe, taped windows that broke and became flying weapons, nor did she experience the untaped windows that were relatively safe. She had only paid attention to "her experience," the shaded box on the upper left in the matrix below. Like Ernie, who believed in the protective power of bananas, Susan had never questioned her belief in the protective powers of masking tape.

WINDOW	DID NOT BREAK	BROKE
WAS TAPED	SAFE: Susan's experience	UNSAFE: Outside of Susan's experience
WAS NOT TAPED	SAFE: What Susan ignored	RELATIVELY SAFE: Outside of Susan's experience

Critical thinkers have developed the mental habit of exploring all four quadrants when they hear a claim like, "I know three people who lost weight using special magnets," or "My father cured his depression by eating beef jerky." Think of the people who did *not* lose weight using special magnets, the people who lost weight *without* the magnets, and the people who *didn't* lose weight and *didn't* use magnets. Think of the people who ate beef jerky and *stayed* depressed, the people who recovered from depression *without* beef jerky, and the people who remain depressed *without* beef jerky. The habit of critical thinking reveals all sorts of mental mistakes—in ourselves and others.

As you observe the benefits of critical thinking in the stories of Clever Hans and facilitated communication, you may find yourself thinking, "Well, of course I wouldn't have fallen for those ridiculous ideas." But that seductive sense of superiority is just another mind bug, and it has a name: the "not-me fallacy."[3]

It can happen to all of us, including your authors. For example, we may be victims of perceiving an illusory correlation between the cases of Clever Hans and facilitated communication. Our view of the past is colored by our experience of the present, a mind bug historians refer to as **presentism,** similar to the mind bug that psychologists call the **hindsight bias.** Imagine a world without critical thinking: No one would ever change his or her mind. Knowledge grows when scientists go out on a limb, hand people the saw of the scientific method, and challenge anyone in the world to use it to make us fall.

We need to think critically about our virtues as well as our faults. For example, one of the most striking parallels between the two stories in this book—the stories of Clever Hans and of facilitated communication—is the sincerity of its advocates. Both the owner of that special horse (Wilhelm von Osten) and the talented, passionate advocate for people with disabilities (Professor Douglas Biklen) appeared to have noble intentions and were idealistically energized by worthy causes (respectively, animal rights and the dignity of people with disabilities). Clever Hans and facilitated communication also have similar back stories. Both rose from obscure beginnings and took their social worlds by storm. They were both aided by sloppy journalism and vivid, entertaining, and inspiring public demonstrations *before* the scientific community had the opportunity to investigate their claims. The advocates for each cause craved the validation of experts and sought the stamp of scientific approval. When science failed to cooperate, both von Osten and Biklen invented increasingly far-fetched explanations for why the judgment of science had to be wrong. When the glaring flaws in both ideas were revealed, their advocates licked their

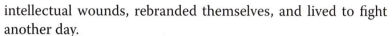

intellectual wounds, rebranded themselves, and lived to fight another day.

Even their techniques bear a striking resemblance. Clever Hans was trained to tap his hoof on the ground; people with autism and other disabilities were guided to tap their fingers on a letter board. Both von Osten and the 20th-century facilitators were convinced that they played no role in controlling the movements of their subjects—even though science unambiguously demonstrated otherwise. Clever Hans and facilitated communication were both "Wow!" events that were intuitively convincing. Who needed scientific proof when the truth was right before your eyes?

The benefits of clear, critical thinking are far more important than Bert, Ernie, and a banana; the social benefits reach far beyond protecting people from flying glass in a storm. We need to be clear, critical thinkers because when we humans make mental mistakes, they are sometimes big mistakes—errors that waste billions of dollars on false ideas, phony medications, bad business decisions, and well-intentioned social interventions that don't work.

The stories of Clever Hans and facilitated communication, troubling as they are, demonstrate how psychology can help us to recognize, and ultimately combat, this problem. In this respect, our book is a story of hope. It teaches us that science, although far from perfect, is ultimately our best safeguard against being fooled, and against unknowingly fooling others. Making psychological science available to the public—and helping people apply it to their daily lives—is why we wrote this book.

CHAPTER 1

Krall, Karl. *Denkende Tiere: Beitrage zur Tierseelenkunde auf Grund eigener Versuche.* Leipzig: Engelmann, 1912, p. 22.

Clever Hans: The Horse That Won't Go Away

Man prefers to believe what man prefers to be true.

Francis Bacon (1561–1626)

Some stories need to be retold to each generation. The story of Clever Hans, the horse that won't go away, is one of them.

As the calendar was turning its centennial page from the 19th to the 20th century, a retired teacher of mathematics named Wilhelm von Osten was working on a project that gave his life a special meaning: teaching his horse to think. It was an odd location for such a momentous undertaking. Von Osten lived alone on the fifth floor of an apartment on Griebenow Street in Berlin, Germany. The apartment looked down on a small, decaying courtyard where he kept his horse, Clever Hans.[1] No one important knew what he was doing, and no one else seemed to care.

The Man and His Mission

The neighbors probably thought of von Osten as the crazy man of the neighborhood; they would lean out their windows and laugh at the elderly bachelor when he led his horse to stand in front of a table, a blackboard, or a row of colored scarves. Von Osten addressed questions directly to Clever Hans, usually standing just behind the horse's right eye. The Russian trotting stallion seemed to answer those questions by shaking his great head, picking up colored scarves with his mouth, and pawing the ground. Small boys on the rooftops made jokes as they watched the bearded gentleman in his long coat and slouch hat. But like all great dreamers, von Osten was not easily deterred. And those same neighbors probably stopped laughing a few years later when the famous horseman Major General Zobel strode into their courtyard. After Zobel's visit, it wasn't long before the "crazy" schoolmaster and his horse were being interviewed, photographed, and discussed in newspapers around the world. Why? Because scientists, horse trainers, and spectators all seemed to confirm what von Osten had been telling people all along: He really had taught his horse to think.

A few critics charged von Osten with fraud, but for all his shortcomings (among them stubbornness, as we will see), the schoolmaster was an honorable man. He could have charged a great deal of money to display Clever Hans, but he never did. He allowed others to work with his horse and under any conditions they cared to create. He often meddled with their experiments—especially when those experiments were not turning out as he had expected. But his belief in his horse was as strong as it was sincere.

Wilhelm von Osten was probably a drill sergeant of a math teacher. He was described as having an "eccentric mind . . . crammed full of theories."[2] He had even preserved the skull of an earlier horse (also named Hans) because he believed that the so-called science of **phrenology** (the analysis of head bumps as a means of detecting people's psychological traits) would one day validate the intelligence of this previous Hans. At some point, however, von Osten must have grown discouraged because he placed an unusual advertisement in both a civilian and military newspaper; it offered a 7-year-old stallion for sale that could distinguish between ten colors and knew the four rules of arithmetic.[3] There were probably no takers to this unusual advertisement because a year later, a smaller advertisement appeared inviting readers to observe—at no charge—demonstrations of the mental powers of horses.

Von Osten wanted his demonstration of Clever Hans's intelligence to be his great contribution to science—and it was, but not in the ways that he had anticipated. Instead, he modeled for future generations how *not* to think. In particular, von Osten demonstrated the dangers of the **confirmation bias:** our tendency to pay attention only to information that confirms what we already believe.

Systematic errors in our thinking are sometimes called "mind bugs" and confirmation bias seems to be one of the most common forms of flawed thinking. For example, von Osten started with a sincere belief that Clever Hans could think like a human, so he only saw evidence that supported his belief. "If my horse makes a big arc in the street in order to turn into a gateway on the other side," he reasoned, then there must be "an autonomous thought process which is capable of being trained."[4] Confirmation bias also takes advantage of our deepest wishes and Clever Hans gave meaning to this last chapter of von Osten's life. He was a bachelor with few friends, a lifetime of experience teaching mathematics, and a deep desire to make a lasting contribution to science. In addition, confirmation bias leaves little room for doubt. The historical record suggests that von Osten experienced doubt about Clever Hans only once and that it lasted less than 24 hours. The inner confidence that comes with confirmation bias probably made it easier for von Osten, after fame came to his courtyard, to say no to a vaudeville company that offered him a *monthly* fee of 30,000 to 60,000 marks (an estimated $100,000 in today's money). When General Zobel responded to that last advertisement during the early summer of 1904, it meant that a recognized expert was confirming his extraordinary claims. The old schoolmaster's tattered dream was finally about to come true.

"So what?" you might say to yourself. "I know my dog thinks because he plans ahead how to steal food from the table—and even seems to experience some version of shame when caught. And I *know* that my cat is thinking; I'm just not sure *what* my cat is thinking." But Clever Hans caught the world of early 20th-century Germany by surprise.

Beware of "Expert" Opinions

History would probably have ignored Clever Hans if von Osten hadn't placed his second, smaller advertisement in a military newspaper. But that advertisement caught the attention of retired Major General Zobel. General Zobel's opinion mattered because he was known as an authority on horses. And horses mattered because the Clever Hans affair unfolded in the technologically exciting decade prior to World War I. Motor cars were becoming common, the Wright brothers' aeroplane had flown 120 feet, and no one had yet imagined dropping bombs from flying machines, building an armored tank, or using chlorine and mustard gas as weapons. A first-rate cavalry, however, was believed to be essential to a nation's military might.[5]

But how could anyone know whether Clever Hans was all that von Osten claimed? Appeals to an authority like General Zobel are persuasive but don't really settle the issue. However, if seeing is believing, then Clever Hans seemed real enough. The horse could accurately tap out an answer to how many "of the gentlemen present are wearing straw hats?" and omit the number of straw hats worn by ladies.[6] He could count the number of windows in distant buildings and the number of children playing on their rooftops. The horse could even calculate the value of German coins.

These displays of intelligence, of course, could all be tricks but the subtle, intuitive details must have impressed General Zobel even more than the counting. For example, anyone could walk right up to Hans and ask questions such as, "How much is $\frac{2}{5}$ plus $\frac{1}{2}$?" Clever Hans would tap out $\frac{9}{10}$ by tapping out the numerator before the denominator. Clever Hans could also calculate square roots and tap out the factors of 28: 2, 4, 7, 14, 28. He carried the yearly calendar in his head, remembered the names of most of the people he had met, and could recognize people from photographs—even when those photographs had been taken some years earlier and bore "but slight resem-blance."[7] Clever Hans also had perfect pitch and a clear sense of musical intervals, and could tap his hoof to indicate which note to remove in order to resolve a dissonant chord. He preferred old-fashioned music from the previous century to the modern tunes popular around 1900.

General Zobel's expert intuition must have vibrated with confirmation bias after observing Clever Hans because the general published his observations in a supplement to one of the daily Berlin newspapers. One can imagine the gossip that flew among the apartments around the dismal courtyard on Griebenow Street. "General Zobel was *here*? In *our* courtyard! *The* General Zobel? To see *von Osten*?!" A duke appeared in the courtyard on Griebenow Street shortly after the general's visit, followed by top army officers, scientists, and larger, ad-miring crowds. Those formerly mocking neighbors testified to reporters that yes, von Osten had treated his horse like a hu-man pupil hour after hour, day after day, for four years. More experts arrived daily: the naturalist and African explorer Pro-fessor G. Schweinfurth, zoologists Dr. O. Heinroth, Dr. Schäff, and K. Möbius, plus another highly regarded horseman, Major R. Schoenbeck.

There was no Internet, of course, to spread the word, but the public endorsement from General Zobel had stirred up plen-ty of attention. Psychologist Oskar Pfungst, a scientist soon to become a key player in the Clever Hans drama, observed that "a flood of articles appeared in the newspapers and magazines" about Clever Hans. There were also "popular couplets and his name was sung on the vaudeville stage."[8] Clever Hans's image appeared on picture postcards and liquor labels, and he was reincarnated in children's toys. This was the moment when von Osten could have cashed in on his equine sensation. But von Osten only wanted to be recognized for his lasting contribution to science. Fortunately for von Osten, a respected scientific authority was about to endorse the amazing Clever Hans.

Professor C. G. Schillings was Germany's famous Indiana Jones-like zoologist and African explorer. He wrote compelling accounts of his adventures, such as losing control of a boat while "drifting irresistibly down-stream toward some rapids. Below these, a number of crocodiles were waiting to receive us with open jaws."[9] But behind the popular drama was a scientist who started taking nighttime photographs of exotic animals and warned people about the growing destruction of the natural world, calling it "the tragedy in the path of progress and civilization." In July 1904 a skeptical Schillings came to Griebenow Street and worked alone with Clever Hans. To his amazement, Clever Hans provided correct answers to unanticipated questions and Schillings sent an enthusiastic report to the August meeting of the Sixth International Congress of Zoologists in Switzerland. Clever Hans had gained scientific credibility from an internationally recognized expert. If your beliefs can be influenced by appeals to authorities, then you probably would have believed in Clever Hans.

The Great Debate: Who Are We?

There was, however, an undercurrent of profound discomfort beneath the acclaim for Clever Hans. It wasn't just that Clever Hans appeared to think, it was that the horse demonstrated astonishing intellectual abilities, at times toying with his audiences in a playful, humanlike way. For example, one questioner grew frustrated when Clever Hans kept tapping his hoof twice rather than the three times required by a correct answer. "And now are you going to answer correctly?" the exasperated questioner demanded of the horse. To the delight of observers, Clever Hans promptly shook his head, "No."

A thinking horse disturbed people in other ways that were difficult to put into words, and one way we humans react to vague threats is to make a joke out of them. In a 1984 study of Clever Hans, Harvard psychologist Dodge Fernald reported a joke that was making the rounds in 1904. A writer to a Berlin newspaper suggested that we humans could "pack up our wisdom and with every passing coach horse doff our hats respectfully." Nearly a century later, comedian Jerry Seinfeld imagined what an alien to planet Earth might think when observing a human walking a dog and cleaning up behind it. Who would you assume is in charge?

The social drama of Clever Hans played out on a philosophically bloody battlefield: the ancient war between superstition and science—even though most people probably did not know what they were fighting about when they discussed Clever Hans. Faith traditions were caught up in the conflict, too, because Genesis 1:26 clearly stated that humans were meant to be in charge of animals. The subtext in the Clever Hans affair was whether humans occupied a special place in creation. "At last," commented Carl Stumpf in his introduction to Pfungst's book, "the thing so long sought for was apparently found. . . ."[10] That was the philosophical sore spot in the great debate: Clever Hans threatened to topple humans from their perch of uniqueness.

Clever Hans also upset some believers in **extrasensory perception (ESP)** because Pfungst rejected ESP as a possible explanation. However, Clever Hans delighted educators (who believed in von Osten's teaching methods) and Darwinists (who believed that Hans demonstrated continuity between species). Clever Hans also resolved a centuries-long philosophical debate about animal consciousness: "This wonderful horse," wrote Oskar Pfungst, "was the means of deciding in the affirmative the old, old, question of the rationality of the lower forms. . . ."[11]

The Clever Hans affair also brought to the surface a not-so-hidden debate about *how* we know what we think we know. One side of that debate is anchored by faith in our intuition. For many people, Clever Hans was nothing short of astounding—and many scientists were just as dazzled as the general public. Their collective intuition was that seeing is believing—a mind bug called **naïve realism.** The other side is anchored by philosopher Sir Karl Popper's **falsification principle;** Popper understood that sometimes **believing is seeing**—that is, when we have decided to believe something, we see what we want to see, and what we want to see is confirmation of our preconceived belief.

Popper's falsification principle is like so-called reality television that gets rid of its potential lovers and survivors—but with one critical difference. In science, you don't get to vote the truth off the island or defer to some famous person's supposedly expert opinion. Like the eventual championship team during the playoffs, the winner in science is the last team—or theory—still standing after many carefully monitored contests called experiments. Science thrives on these experimental contests between ideas and knows that another contender is always waiting in the wings, eager to supplant the accepted wisdom of the day. According to Popper's falsification approach, even the best corroborated of theories—Charles Darwin's elegant theory of evolution by means of natural selection or the Big Bang theory of the origin of the universe—will be discarded if they can be disproved.

We humans seem to have inherited an impulse to think in terms of confirmation rather than falsification. So, as the Berlin spring of 1904 gave way to summer, it seemed like all the experts and the audiences coming to Griebenow Street were in agreement that Mr. von Osten had been right all along. And that meant that a lot of different people and groups might have to change what they believed. That is why Clever Hans poses such a universally disturbing question: What will we do when the evidence contradicts what we already believe?

The "Hans Commission"

When some people cried fraud against von Osten and Schillings, von Osten asked the Berlin Board of Education to convene, in effect, a court of honor to examine his methods.[12] Von Osten wanted to settle the issue once and for all, and Schillings had a scientific reputation to protect. Von Osten wanted a panel of experts to put a grand stamp of scientific confirmation on the great mission of his life. To his disappointment, the Berlin Board of Education chose to stay out of the debate but others were eager to investigate—including Professor Carl Stumpf from the new science of psychology. The voluntary group brought distinctive skills to a narrow purpose: to act as a court of honor on behalf of von Osten and Schillings. It was an impressive, eclectic commission that should have been able to detect any ongoing trickery:

Paul Busch, circus manager

Otto, Count of Castell-Rüdenhausen

Dr. A. Grabow, member of the school board, retired

Robert Hahn, teacher, municipal schools

Dr. Ludwig Heck, director of the Berlin Zoological Garden

Dr. Oskar Heinroth, assistant in the Berlin Zoological Garden

Dr. Richard Kandt

Major F. W. von Keller, retired

Major-General Th. Köring, retired

Dr. Miessner, assistant in the Royal Veterinary College

Professor Nagel, head of the Department of Sense-Physiology at the Physiological Institute of the University of Berlin

Professor C. Stumpf, director of the Berlin Psychological Institute, member of the Academy of Science

Henry Suermondt

Each member of the group was assigned to closely observe a different part of von Osten's body as he asked Clever Hans questions. One person watched von Osten's head, another his eyes or right hand, left hand, and so forth. Busch, the circus manager, was the sole exception because of his greater experience with training animals. He chose to observe the questioner's overall behavior and sometimes shifted his attention to watch the audience. Clever Hans passed all their tests with flying colors. He tapped the numbers representing the days of the week, the date, and solutions to a variety of arithmetic problems. He even spelled out the name of the circus manager. It did not matter whether von Osten or Schillings asked the questions; Clever Hans was almost 100% accurate.

The members of the commission unanimously agreed that they had not witnessed any intentional signaling. But that was not the story that got picked up by the newspapers. The headline appearing on October 2, 1904 in *The New York Times* was based on an article published in *The London Standard*:

> "'CLEVER HANS' AGAIN. Expert Commission
> Decides That the Horse Actually Reasons."

Of course, the informal, volunteer committee had not reached the conclusion proclaimed in the headline. Then, as now, scientists and headline writers have different agendas—the former to test hypotheses, and the latter to attract readers. Carl Stumpf's report and later introduction to Pfungst's book about Clever Hans went to great lengths to correct misperceptions about the findings of the so-called Hans Commission. But to the international audience now following the story, General Zobel, C. G. Schillings, and a prestigious commission all agreed that Clever Hans could think. Scientific psychology is still fighting those same battles. News reports, movies, and television drama often promote public *mis*perceptions of psychological findings.[13] Life would be much easier if we could trust experts, blue ribbon commissions, and news reports, but we can't.

Climbing the Wrong Mountain

Imagine the effort. Like hikers following blaze markings up a steep mountain trail, the retired schoolmaster was guiding Hans step by step into higher levels of learning. There was only one problem: Von Osten had started up the wrong trail. All his efforts had taken him to the top of Mount Self-Deception rather than Mount Achievement.

Here is what von Osten thought was happening.

The schoolteacher had kept Clever Hans on a lean diet. Hans was always hungry, so it was easy to use food as a reward as von Osten taught him to tap his hoof. At the beginning, this required that von Osten bend over to lift Hans's hoof and then straighten up again to feed him. In von Osten's mind, Clever Hans's tapping became counting and counting led to arithmetic. For example, von Osten placed a single wooden pin on a table in front of Hans and then commanded him: "Raise the foot!—One!" As soon as Hans tapped once, von Osten turned and gave Clever Hans some food. Then it was "Raise the foot! —One—Two!" and so forth.[14] As they slowly progressed through levels of arithmetic, von Osten used traditional teaching methods and devices such as wooden pins, a counting machine commonly used in the schools, charts with numbers, and large digits made of brass that hung from a string. At the beginning of Hans's education in numbers, the teaching method was a slow, systematic march to the ultimate goal: a horse that could think for himself.

Clever Hans was at first a slow learner. But later on, von Osten explained to Pfungst, he allowed Clever Hans "to discover a great deal for himself." As they moved deeper into the mysteries of mathematics, von Osten reported that "Hans had to develop the multiplication table for himself."[15] Von Osten then connected the idea of a number to a written number drawn on a chalkboard, followed by a table that transformed number combinations into letters. Letters were combined into words, words into ideas, and ideas into a conversation. There seemed to be only one possible explanation: Clever Hans was *thinking*.

The little details were especially convincing. Clever Hans tapped faster when he had to tap out a large number, as if eager to complete a boring task. Sometimes Hans would add one more tap with his left hoof, like an exclamation mark. The horse, like his master, seemed to have a touchy personality. Hans did not seem to like Carl Stumpf, for example, and sometimes bit him. Occasionally, the hungry horse even bit von Osten or ran wildly around the courtyard. But he always came back for another morsel of food. Even Clever Hans's temper made sense, though, because learning can be hard, frustrating work. That is what von Osten believed was happening. Everything fit together in the schoolteacher's tidy world of confirmation bias.

Here is what was really happening.

Clever Hans had figured out two things: (1) If he wanted any food, then he better start tapping his hoof whenever von Osten leaned forward. (2) He could only stop tapping and expect some food when von Osten started to look up. Von Osten was watching Clever Hans's hoof, while Clever Hans was watching von Osten's head.

An accidental signal from von Osten to his horse is a very simple explanation, but it still accounts for all the evidence. Scientists try to explain things using the simplest possible theory—and no simpler, a goal goes by several names, including **parsimony** and the **principle of least astonishment (POLA)**. Explanations that are as simple as possible—and no simpler—can protect us from the subtle process of self-deception. For example, it seemed entirely natural for von Osten to lean forward to watch Hans's hoof and then look up to feed his horse. It was such a natural thing to do that even von Osten did not realize that he was sending Hans a signal. The crowds that came to witness the extraordinary horse did the same thing. They also would ask a question, lean forward to watch Hans's hoof, and then lean back in amazement when the horse tapped out the correct number. It was a case of pure, **spontaneous self-deception.**

By mid-summer the crowds coming to Griebenow Street grew quite large. But the thought of charging money never seemed to occur to von Osten. Indeed, anyone could walk into the courtyard around noon, when von Osten started his daily demonstrations. If von Osten was called away, then visitors could go right up to Clever Hans and ask him questions. Of course, the visitors would lean forward, stare intently at Hans's hoof, and then straighten up in amazement. Clever Hans's arithmetic was less reliable when he was uncertain about who was asking the questions, but some 40 people reliably asked and obtained correct answers from the horse. Sometimes the sessions went late into the evening and Clever Hans's performance declined as the shadows lengthened. But it seemed reasonable to attribute those errors to fatigue after a long day's work. After all, the horse was only—well, almost—human.

Wilhelm von Osten had climbed the wrong mountain and he had taken many people with him.

Clear Thinking Is Critical Thinking

There is a hero in the story of Clever Hans and his name is Oskar Pfungst. Although Carl Stumpf designed some of the experiments, it was Pfungst, Stumpf's student and colleague at the Berlin Psychological Institute, who did the heavy lifting. Mr. von Osten soon came to wish that he had never invited those two scientific truth tellers into his courtyard. Pfungst devised a plan that would rule out rival explanations.

You may be familiar with the idea of **ruling out** if you or someone you know has wrestled with a difficult medical diagnosis. You may think, for example, that you have a bad case of poison ivy, but then hear your doctor say, "Well, we can rule out poison ivy. Your rash is fairly smooth and shaped like a target. A rash from poison ivy is typically streaky and red, has bumps, and sometimes fluid-filled blisters." Your physician does not yet know what your problem is, but can tell you what your problem probably is *not*—she or he has falsified or ruled out the poison ivy hypothesis.

One of the most tempting alternative hypotheses about Clever Hans was **telepathy** (or **thought transference**), an interpretation that Sigmund Freud also found appealing. Freud encouraged a friend to observe the horse for a couple of weeks and then write about it.[16] Telepathy also made sense if you trusted your own experience to be your guide. For example, Pfungst noticed that "as soon as I concentrated my attention upon the number he promptly responded correctly."[17] Wow! More concentration equals better communication. Isn't that telepathy? Pfungst later observed that all he had to do was focus "consciousness, with a great degree of intensity, upon the answer desired."[18] Double wow! That certainly sounds like telepathy. "The animal always followed the ideas which were in the questioner's mind," Pfungst reported, "and never his words."[19] Triple wow!

Telepathy could even explain Clever Hans's failures: Either the horse or the human wasn't concentrating hard enough, or not operating on the same psychic wavelength. Perhaps the horse had even switched psychic channels—so to speak—to make a telepathic connection with someone else in the audience. Even Oskar Pfungst acknowledged that, "from the very beginning Hans responded as promptly to those questions which I articulated merely inwardly, as to those which were spoken aloud."[20] Now isn't that scientific proof? Isn't that an example of thought transmission? And isn't mysterious communication between minds what psychology is really all about?

No.

No.

No.

That is not scientific evidence. It is not a demonstration of thought transmission. And it is the *opposite* of what scientific psychology is all about. It will take just a little more effort to understand why, but the extra effort should not surprise us. Clear, critical thinking requires more conscious effort than "going with our gut."

Oskar Pfungst demonstrated clear, critical thinking by organizing experiments around the **method of elimination,** so he could systematically rule out **alternative explanations.** He used procedures that made it easy for Clever Hans to succeed. For example, he erected a large canvas tent to minimize visual distractions and prevent the curious public from interfering. Pfungst also conducted many versions of the same experiment "in order to obviate the possibility of the . . . horse's answers due to chance."[21] In addition, Pfungst worried about tiring Hans with long sessions. Errors due to fatigue should not be counted as evidence against the horse's intelligence. Pfungst designed experiments that gave Clever Hans the best opportunity to

TABLE 1.1: Clear Thinking About Clever Hans.

It was easy to deceive yourself about Clever Hans if you only paid attention to the cell in the upper right-hand corner labeled CONFIRMATION BIAS.

CLEVER HANS	HANS DID NOT TAP THE CORRECT NUMBER	TAPPED THE CORRECT NUMBER
"WITH KNOWLEDGE"	This happened occasionally, but von Osten always had explanations.	CONFIRMATION BIAS This happened frequently and got everyone excited about Clever Hans.
"WITHOUT KNOWLEDGE"	This happened frequently after Stumpf and Pfungst designed tests that Hans could fail.	This never happened except by chance.

succeed. That is one way that scientific procedures represent our best, but still imperfect, safeguard against self-deception.

To test whether Hans was being signaled, Pfungst conducted a series of simple tests that he called **with knowledge** and **without knowledge.** Clever Hans was shown numbers on a series of cards. In one condition, the questioner was positioned so that both the questioner and Clever Hans could see the number on the card (with knowledge). In another condition, the questioner was positioned so that only Clever Hans could see the number on the card (without knowledge). The experiments summarized in Table 1.1 answered two crucial questions: Can Clever Hans solve mathematical problems or read and understand the German language? Pfungst reported some of those results in the following table:

METHOD	THE NUMBER DISPLAYED ON CARD	THE NUMBER TAPPED BY CLEVER HANS
Without knowledge	8	14
With knowledge	8	8
Without knowledge	4	8
With knowledge	4	4
Without knowledge	7	9
With knowledge	7	7
Without knowledge	10	17
With knowledge	10	10
Without knowledge	3	9
With knowledge	3	3

During 49 tests without knowledge, Clever Hans tapped out the correct answer only 8% of the time. Over 42 tests with knowledge, he tapped out the correct answer 98% of the time. One doesn't need a fancy statistical test to interpret those numbers. There were also 26 tests of Clever Hans's ability to read simple words. Clever Hans's rate of correct answers with knowledge was 100%; without knowledge 0%. When testing whether Clever Hans could understand human speech and compute numbers, the horse pawed the correct number on 29 out of 31 tests with knowledge, but only 3 out of 31 times on tests without knowledge. All the results told the same story: Clever Hans could not compute numbers, understand or read German, recognize colors, or identify musical notes or chords. Clever Hans was being signaled.

But how was Clever Hans being signaled?

What About Intuition and Telepathy?

Many people trust their **intuition** as a reliable way of knowing and making major life decisions. We have to trust our intuition: We meet too many people every day to stop and analyze every interaction. But intuition can also lead us astray. Pfungst observed that even "sober-minded folk" intuitively perceived indicators of genius in Clever Hans's "intelligent eye, the high forehead, the carriage of the head, which clearly showed a 'real thought process was going on inside'."[22] One report declared that "Hans turned appreciatively toward visitors who made some remark in praise of his accomplishments."[23] That would have been a sublime moment for the person looking back at Hans. "The horse looked directly at me. I connected with him! Brain to brain! I could feel it. You'll never be able to tell me otherwise." But that's the nature of intuitions, both true and false. A feeling can be real even though the idea that produced that feeling can be false. All we have to do is believe.

Pfungst suspected that Hans was being signaled by some visual cue. So he placed large blinders on Clever Hans's face that prevented the horse from seeing the questioner: Hans immediately began to twist and turn violently, trying to see the questioner—something he had never done before. In the 35 trials when the questioner was not seen, Clever Hans tapped out the correct answer only 6% of the time. In the 56 cases in which the questioner was seen, Clever Hans tapped out the correct answer 89% of the time. In the 11 cases labeled undecided because of all the twisting and turning, Clever Hans tapped out the correct answer 18% of the time. The telepathy hypothesis appeared to be incorrect because physical blinders should not have interfered with thought transmission. Even though an entire commission of experts had carefully observed von Osten, it required controlled experiments to "see" what humans could not perceive: Clever Hans needed to see the questioner to answer questions correctly.

Suddenly, other observations began to make sense. For example, when Hans approached the correct number of taps, he would start to make one more tap but then stop, as if he had calculated one number too high and then thought better of it. Clever Hans also had difficulty answering questions when the correct answer was the number 1. Pfungst realized, "Hans never knows in advance which tap is to be the final one."[24] Another peculiarity was that Clever Hans would start tapping whenever Pfungst bent forward slightly to write in his notebook. None of those observations made any sense until you knew how Hans was being signaled.

Over the years, von Osten's movements had become so subtle that none of the "thousands of spectators, horse-fanciers, trick-trainers of first rank [could] discover any kind of signal."[25] Even a slight dilation of the questioner's nostrils or raising of the eyebrows could signal the hungry horse, usually "accompanied by some slight involuntary upward movement of the head."[26] Bending over even more made Hans tap even faster. In one experiment, Pfungst asked Clever Hans to tap out the number 13 while consciously (and with difficulty) keeping his own head tilted forward. Hans kept right on tapping until he reached the number 20, when Pfungst finally lifted his head again. Across 26 such tests, Clever Hans tapped past the number requested every time and did not stop tapping until the questioner had finally lifted his head. Again, no statistics are needed.

Pfungst compared these involuntary movements to a bowler who is concentrating on bowling a strike. Some people wave at the ball; others twist their bodies; some even shuffle onto the neighboring lane—without being conscious of their own behavior. Try it for yourself by concentrating *with increasing intensity* as you look at your feet: Your muscles tense, your eyebrows narrow, and your head, of course, has to look down. Now try arching your eyebrows and looking around you: Your head automatically lifts upward, especially if you have been watching something on the ground with great intensity.

What about the telepathy hypothesis? Remember, blinders should not have interfered with thought transmission. Still, isn't it possible that some people just have the gift? Pfungst himself reported that "I usually had a feeling when Hans had arrived at the right number."[27] Pfungst put himself in the role of the horse and tapped his finger while other people concentrated on some number. He tested 25 different people "of every age and sex . . . differing also in nationality and occupation." None of them knew the purpose of the study, yet 23 out of the 25 people he tested made the same "sudden slight upward jerk of the head when the final number was reached."[28] When he asked people to think of "up," "down," "right," and "left," they moved their heads in the corresponding direction. Pfungst conducted 350 tests using 12 different participants and made an average of 73% correct responses, so he was not quite as good as Clever Hans. But Pfungst had not been practicing for his food every day for four years.

Try it for yourself with some unsuspecting friend. You will probably have to practice a little to find the best rate of finger tapping, but it won't take you four years to learn the trick. Your friend may suspect that you have the gift of telepathy. Please don't deceive them: Be a scientist about it, explain that you got the idea from a horse, and then tell them the story of Clever Hans.

After-the-Fact (Post-Hoc) Explanations

No one set out to deceive or commit fraud. Oskar Pfungst acknowledged that even he was not "aware of my own movements" when signaling the horse "until I had noted those of Mr. von Osten." It was, Pfungst concluded, "a case of pure self-deception."[29] But once you know the simple explanation of visual cueing, you start to realize that believing in Clever Hans required blind faith in many small but ridiculous beliefs, such as:

1. Von Osten had the skill and wisdom to teach a horse how to think.

2. Clever Hans could learn written and spoken German very quickly.

3. Clever Hans *wanted* to express his intelligence in public.

4. Clever Hans could see straight ahead and for long distances.

5. Clever Hans had developed musical preferences for music that he had never heard.

6. Clever Hans learned mathematical concepts faster than most humans.

7. Clever Hans had learned French by overhearing French visitors.

It all seems so obvious after the fact. That's when we all fall prey to the **Texas sharpshooter fallacy,** named after the proverbial person who shoots holes in the barn wall and later draws target circles around the holes. In hindsight, it looks like every shot was a bull's-eye. Von Osten resorted to increasingly strange, untestable explanations for Clever Hans's failures but they still made sense to him. Von Osten claimed that Clever Hans was tired; Clever Hans was stubborn; Clever Hans just wasn't in the mood to answer questions correctly. But the schoolmaster's most desperate explanation was that "the sensitive animal could easily perceive the questioner's ignorance and would therefore lose confidence in, and respect for, him."[30] That's right: Von Osten even claimed that Clever Hans disdained to answer questions from people whose intelligence he recognized as inferior to his own!

So that was it. A series of elegant, controlled experiments explained a phenomenon that had upset the Church, annoyed the psychics, drawn the praise of educators, encouraged the Darwinists, convinced famous scientists, inspired a prominent military general, befuddled a committee of experts, captured international headlines, raised a philosophical conundrum, and provoked a passionate public debate. Clever Hans was just a hungry horse responding to subtle, unintentional head movements. Oskar Pfungst wrote, "It seems almost ridiculous that this should never have been noticed before"[31] Wilhelm von Osten had led a large group of sloppy (uncritical) thinkers to the top of Mount Self-Deception. But would he admit it? Would you?

For humans who look to psychology for answers in the 21st century, this is the turning point when the story of Clever Hans shifts from entertaining to disturbing to dangerous.

Two Cases of Cognitive Dissonance

When Pfungst's blinder experiments disproved von Osten's cherished belief, the schoolmaster was first of all surprised. But then he displayed a "tragi-comic rage directed against the horse."[32] Von Osten's suddenly wonderful world had changed back again, and into something even worse. At first, however, he seemed to accept the judgment of science and told Carl Stumpf and Oskar Pfungst, "The gentlemen must admit that after seeing the objective success of my efforts at instruction, I was warranted in my belief." But something happened as von Osten mulled things over that night because the next day he "was as ardent an exponent of the belief in the horse's intelligence as he ever had been."[33]

What made von Osten change his mind during that long, soul-searching night? The most likely answer is **cognitive dissonance**: the distress we experience when we hold incompatible beliefs. Think about his situation. He was "an old man," Pfungst wrote, "unmarried and entirely alone . . . and his Hans was almost his sole companion."[34] The night after the blinder experiment, von Osten probably sat alone in his fifth-floor apartment while his thoughts ping-ponged back and forth. "Clever Hans can think." "No, he can't." "But I never tried to signal him." "Nevertheless, you've been signaling Hans all along." "But even experts believe in Clever Hans—General Zobel, Schillings, the Commission. . . ." "Hans couldn't answer the simplest question when he had the blinders on." "But I've spent so many years following my dream, even when people laughed at me. . . ." Who of us could live with so much dissonance about something so important to our lives? Von Osten tried to find mental peace by insisting that he had been right about Clever Hans all along.

Shortly after the blinder experiment, Mr. von Osten wrote a brief note to Carl Stumpf "in which he forbade further experimentation with the horse." Why? "The purpose of our inquiries," von Osten explained, "had been to corroborate his theories"[35]: the very definition of the confirmation bias. Pfungst's experiments had created cognitive dissonance by systematically taking the legs out from under the belief system endorsed so publicly by von Osten and Professor Schillings.

However, the two men escaped from their cognitive dissonance in starkly different ways, and with very different consequences. Von Osten continued to believe in Clever Hans but refused to allow any more experiments. In contrast, Schillings not only changed his mind, he told others to watch von Osten's head movements during Clever Hans's demonstrations. Von Osten chose to ignore or reinterpret the evidence. Schillings did not try to change the evidence; he let the evidence change him. He had to overcome his confirmation bias and publically admit that he had been wrong. Precious few of us have the intellectual courage to do that, but it is the scientific way.

Von Osten was not a fraud. The rush of international fame may have limited his ability to think critically, but sudden international celebrity would probably have that effect on most of us. He continued to exhibit Clever Hans, but his enthusiasm had been severely dampened by Pfungst's report. As the crowds stopped coming to Griebenow Street, von Osten decided that the scientists were somehow to blame. He came to a sad ending. Wilhelm von Osten was 70 years old when he "died in gloom and solitude"[36] on June 29, 1909, "apparently of a broken heart" and sadly "frustrated in the great goal of his life."[37] In his will, he bequeathed his beloved Clever Hans to Karl Krall, who already owned a stable full of supposedly intelligent horses. As for C. G. Schillings, the famous explorer continued to write books about his adventures in the wild and his use of the new technique of nighttime photography. Those books, however, do not appear to mention the summer of 1904 and Professor Schillings's singular role in the Clever Hans affair.

Oskar Pfungst briefly became a celebrity in Berlin, giving lectures and writing articles for the press.[38] He demonstrated that, contrary to accepted wisdom, horses never responded to verbal commands or bugle calls. Those commands simply co-occurred with signals coming from the rider through the reins, whip, or boots. He tried to investigate Karl Krall's horses but he was rebuffed. Leonard Zusne (1984) reported that Pfungst never received his advanced degree from the Berlin Psychological Institute.[39] His work with Clever Hans has endured, however, and many years later he was awarded an honorary medical degree from the University of Frankfurt.

Beliefs Don't Have to Die

Beliefs, unlike people, don't have to die.

Karl Krall claimed that he had taught his horses (and other animals) more in a few months than what von Osten had taught Clever Hans over four years. But Krall's thinking was crawling with mind bugs. For example, Krall reacted with confirmation bias when his most famous horse Mohammed misspelled someone's name. Krall asked Mohammed to try again . . . and again. When Mohammed still left out certain letters, Krall still credited the horse with having spelled the name correctly because Mohammed had invented phonetic spellings for efficiency's sake. It would be difficult to imagine a better example of an implausible, post-hoc, dissonance-inspired excuse for an impossible belief than a horse using phonetic spelling.

The "experts" around Krall were no help. *Before* the Nobel Prize-winning novelist Maurice Maeterlinck visited Karl Krall's stable, he wrote, "I was wholly persuaded of the genuineness" of the horse's intelligence. Then he looked Mohammed "straight in the eyes . . . in order to catch a sign of his genius."[40] Maurice Maeterlinck may have been a fine novelist, but he was a terrible critical thinker when it came to Krall's beloved horse. He had made up his mind to "see" what he already believed.

People in the United States showed similar enthusiasm for a horse named Beautiful Jim Key that was supposed to be able to read, spell, do arithmetic, and cite Bible passages. Jim Key had his own pavilion at the 1904 World's Fair and became one of its most profitable attractions. Theodore Roosevelt's daughter, Alice, came with her escort Nicholas Longworth. Beautiful Jim

Key spelled out A-L-I-C-E R-O-O-S-E-V-E-L-T . . . and then, to the crowd's delight, the horse added L-O-N-G-W-O-R-T-H. The couple became engaged the following year and shortly thereafter married in a White House ceremony. Would you call that proof of Beautiful Jim Key's abilities?

In the mid-1920s the self-proclaimed psychic C. D. Fonda demonstrated the psychic abilities of her horse Lady Wonder— for three questions per dollar. An editorial in the Richmond, Virginia, *Times-Dispatch* by radio commentator A. C. Griffiths described how he came to believe in Lady Wonder. "The instant I thought of the spelling of my middle name, Lady's head moved to the keyboard and she typed it accurately."[41] He was still describing his experience 50 years later. No controlled experiments were needed; one subjective experience and faith in his intuition were enough.

Lady Wonder's tricks were exposed by two New Jersey magicians, Milbourne Christopher and John Scarne. They discovered that Mrs. Fonda was twitching a small whip to signal Lady Wonder. In one test, Christopher stood some distance from Mrs. Fonda and made a show of moving his pencil in the path of a figure 8 but only touched the paper to write the number 3. Lady Wonder "guessed" the number 8.[42] John Scarne discovered that Lady Wonder could not mind read the answer to a simple question about what state he lived in—until he moved his hand just enough to give Mrs. Fonda a peek at the answer he had written on a piece of paper.[43] Even then, Lady Wonder wrongly reported New York rather than New Jersey.

If we were cynics rather than skeptics, we might conclude that what we learn from history is that we don't learn from history. But psychological science offers a better way: clear, critical thinking. As we will see in Chapter 2, the stakes are higher—much higher—than we might imagine.

Clever Hands: The Facilitated Communication Story

The past is never dead. In fact, it's not even past.

William Faulkner

In all respects, Julian and Thal Wendrow appeared to be a typical middle-class couple. Julian owned a house-painting business, and Thal was an attorney working for a county court judge. Julian had been a resident of South Africa but moved to the United States in the 1980s after falling in love with Thal. The Wendrows settled in West Bloomfield, Michigan, a peaceful suburb outside of Detroit, Michigan, and had two children: a girl, Aislinn, born in 1993, and a boy, Ian, born about a year later.

Yet not long after Ian's birth, as his older sister Aislinn approached the age when children begin to walk and talk, the Wendrows realized that something was not quite right with her. Aislinn had appeared to be a normal infant, but at around 18 months her verbal output began to shrink, and by the age of 2 she barely spoke at all. Shortly thereafter she was diagnosed with **autism** (now formally called **autism spectrum disorder**). Like the behaviors of many people with autism, Aislinn's were often odd and socially inappropriate. When the family went to movies, she often sat in the theater rocking back and forth, moaning. Years later, at school during gym class, she sometimes sat naked by herself in the locker room. As an older child, she displayed minimal interest in interacting with others. By age 14, she remained essentially mute and did not seem to relate well emotionally to her parents or others. Specialists in developmental disabilities diagnosed her as mentally retarded. As most parents in this situation would be, the Wendrows were devastated by Aislinn's deficits. Still, they continued to believe that lurking somewhere within Aislinn was an intelligent, emotionally complex young woman yearning to emerge.

Understandably desperate to connect emotionally with Aislinn, the Wendrows began not only to look into treatment options, but also to become active in the autism treatment community. Julian joined a Michigan organization established to assist individuals with disabilities, and Thal became a board member of the local chapter of the Autism Society of America. After exhausting a host of options, in 2004, they attended a seminar held by Dr. Sandra McClennen, a retired professor of education at nearby Eastern Michigan University. At this seminar, Julian and Thal learned of an intervention called **facilitated communication (FC)** that seemed to be a revolutionary breakthrough in the treatment of autism. It almost seemed too good to be true—but a few professors had become advocates of this new approach since its invention some 25 years earlier. The Wendrows must have wished, "If only it's true. . . ." And who can blame them for wanting the best for their precious child?

Here is how FC works. The nonverbal individual with autism is provided with a computer keyboard or a letter pad. It could even be something as simple as a piece of cardboard that contains the letters of the alphabet. Whatever the device might be, it is usually placed on a table or supported in some way, even held in front of the nonverbal individual. Then, he sits next to an adult facilitator who gently holds and guides his arm and hand as they approach the letters. The facilitator doesn't do any of the "typing," acting only as a steadying influence on the autistic person's upper limb movements so he can become, in effect, a one-fingered typist. Lo and behold, the formerly mute person with autism can now spell out words, phrases, and even complete and meaningful sentences. FC, its advocates maintain, is a portal to a previously undiscovered world, the land of the autistic person's unspoken thoughts.

After attending McClennan's seminar, the Wendrows became ardent advocates of FC. Aislinn's school district, Walled Lake Consolidated, was reluctant to adopt the technique, but Julian and Thal insisted on it. After they threatened to sue the school district, they finally received their much desired facilitator and, with it, renewed hopes for their daughter. What's more, the Wendrows' dream of communicating with Aislinn came true. FC was all they could have hoped for, and more.

As had been reported in many previous cases of nonverbal children who tried FC, Aislinn soon began to type messages of extraordinary eloquence and poignancy. Aislinn was apparently not mentally retarded after all. She wrote of her love for her parents and of her career dreams, including her desire to one day become a college professor. She began taking classes in history, English, and algebra—and performed well in them. She even composed poetry. For more than two years, Aislinn remained verbally uncommunicative, even as she continued to type articulate statements with the assistance of her facilitator.

Like Wilhelm von Osten with his marvelous horse, the Wendrows suddenly confronted the happiest of dilemmas: What do you when your cherished dream starts to come true?

The Voice Mail

One day, in late November 2007, Julian Wendrow received an unexpected voice mail upon returning home from work. The caller, a social worker at the Michigan Department of Human Services, asked that one of Aislinn's parents return the call to discuss a matter pertaining to their daughter's school. When Julian spoke to the social worker, he received a jarring piece of news.

That morning, Aislinn had been communicating with the help of a new FC aide, Cynthia Scarsella, who had acquired all of her knowledge about facilitated communication in a one-hour workshop. Scarsella asked Aislinn how her Thanksgiving weekend with her parents had gone. In response, Aislinn typed a message that caught her teachers' attention. The facilitated message (with typographical errors included) read as follows:

"My dad gets me up banges me and then we have breakfast and I take a shower with his help and start doing homework. He put s his hands on my private parts."

When asked "What do you mean by banges me?," Aislinn responded by typing one word: "Swx." It did not escape the attention of her teachers that *w* is only one letter away from *e* on the keyboard, so the meaning of Aislinn's answer was self-evident. In other facilitated messages, Aislinn wrote that the sexual abuse had been occurring for years, and that Thal was aware of the abuse but did nothing to try to stop it. My mother, she wrote, "pretends not to no."

That night, police arrived at the Wendrows' home and accused Julian of sexually abusing Aislinn, a charge that Julian denied vehemently. Two days later, under questioning by authorities, Aislinn repeated her sexual abuse claims during facilitation with Scarsella. In response, the Michigan Department of Social Services placed both Aislinn and her brother Ian in protective custody. The same day, a nurse examined Aislinn, but found an intact hymen, along with no other clear physical indications of sexual abuse.

By this point, however, the police were quite certain that Julian was guilty. Still, the lone piece of evidence against him was the facilitated allegation of abuse, so they pressed for more information. A few days later, in a grueling 1 hour and 40 minute session in a small, isolated room, police interrogated Aislinn's younger brother Ian in an effort to solicit tangible eyewitness evidence of abuse. When they were unable to get Ian to corroborate the accusations, the police deceived him, informing him falsely that they had videotapes of his father abusing Aislinn. Eventually, under intense pressure, Ian told police that on a few occasions, he had witnessed his father shower with Aislinn while she was nude—a not especially unusual practice for a parent caring for a child with severe intellectual disability, the contemporary term for what was once called mental retardation.

Things only got worse. On December 6th, Aislinn typed a facilitated message alleging that her parents had violated a court order by visiting her. Although this claim later turned out not to be true, the police proceeded to place the Wendrows under arrest. Technically, Julian was jailed on the basis of contempt of court, as he and Thal were accused—yes, on the basis of FC— of attempting to flee the country to escape the charges against them. Julian, held without bond, spent 80 days in jail, 76 of them isolated in a tiny cell. Thal was imprisoned for 5 days on charges of ignoring her daughter's sexual abuse; upon release, she was deemed a flight risk and forced to wear an electronic tether. For at least two months, prosecutors and police doggedly pursued the case against the Wendrows, accruing evidence against them largely in the form of additional facilitated communications from Aislinn.

To defend themselves against these accusations, the Wendrows and several scholarly experts on facilitated communication with whom they consulted demanded a simple experiment. Aislinn would be questioned with a facilitator other than Cynthia Scarsella to determine whether Aislinn's messages could be reproduced using a different aide. The police and prosecutors steadfastly refused. Finally, in late January 2005, the Wendrows' case came before a judge. There, Aislinn was asked about the abuse allegations on the witness stand, with Scarsella present as facilitator. We will learn of the dramatic culmination of this case later in the chapter. For now, it is important to know that the Wendrows' nightmare was hardly the first of its kind, a fact of which they were unaware when they eagerly sought out FC training for their daughter.

As of the mid-1990s, at least 60 legal cases had emerged involving sexual abuse allegations against parents based exclusively on facilitated messages. One 1991 case was eerily similar to that of the Wendrows. Jenny Storch was a 14-year-old living in upstate New York. Like Aislinn, Jenny was essentially mute and had been diagnosed with autism. She, too, had been set up with a facilitator at school, much to the delight of Jenny's parents, Mark and Laura. For a time, FC seemingly introduced them to a deep and loving side of Jenny that they had never known, or even suspected of existing. Yet after Jenny typed a facilitated message alleging over 200 brutal accusations of rape against her father, Jenny was removed from the home, despite the absence of any incriminating physical evidence against Mark Storch. A year later, another case in southern Maine involved a 17-year-old girl with autism named Betsy Wheaton. With the help of a facilitator at school who was using a letter board, Betsy typed out allegations that her mother, father, grandparents, and brother were all abusing her sexually. Based exclusively on these accusations, Betsy was removed from her home and placed in foster care.

Is facilitated communication for real? What lessons can we draw from the Wendrows' disturbing story? And what does their tale tell us about why the ghost of Clever Hans continues to haunt educated, sincere, well-intentioned people? These troubling questions will help us discover how the everyday research tools of psychological science can protect, but not immunize, us against the dangers of spontaneous self-deception.

The Wendrows probably did not fully grasp the network of beliefs that shaped our early understanding of autism. But those early efforts to understand autism, developed by well-regarded authorities, set the stage for the miserable dramas that the Wendrow, Storch, and Wheaton families—and many others—were forced to endure. They also explain why FC continues to shape misguided popular thinking about how to help people with autism.

"Refrigerator" Mothers and Other Stubborn Fictions

The concept of autism, or autism spectrum disorder as it is now called, is a relative newcomer to the lexicon of psychological diagnoses. The term "autism" originated in 1943, when Leo Kanner (pronounced "Conner"), a child psychiatrist at the Johns Hopkins University, published an article entitled "Autistic Disturbances of Affective Contact" in a medical journal. In this article, Kanner meticulously described 11 children whom we would now recognize as displaying unmistakable features of autism.[1] One 5-year-old boy, identified as Donald T., was, in Kanner's words, "happiest when left alone." As Kanner observed, Donald "almost never cried to go with his mother, did not seem to notice his father's homecomings, and was indifferent to visiting relatives."[2] Kanner called the condition "early infantile autism," selecting the prefix "auto" to reflect the profound self-preoccupation of individuals with the condition.

Only a year after Kanner's publication, Austrian pediatrician Hans Asperger (whose name is immortalized in the eponymous Asperger's syndrome, which is now regarded by most scholars as a high-functioning variant of autism) described a strikingly similar spectrum of deficits, even though he was apparently unaware of Kanner's writings. In his vivid case studies, Asperger in 1944[3] wrote of a distinctive syndrome marked by an absence of empathy, preoccupation with highly specific interests, and a lack of interest in others. He referred to children with these symptoms as "little professors," noting that they routinely accumulated astonishing amounts of expertise regarding narrow intellectual topics, such as train schedules or mathematical equations.

Today, the American Psychiatric Association's *Diagnostic and Statistical Manual of Mental Disorders*, (5th ed., known as the DSM–5)[4] describes autism spectrum disorder as a condition that both Kanner and Asperger would have readily recognized. According to the manual, autism is characterized by impairments in two overarching domains: (1) social communication, including a preference for solitary play and disturbances in eye contact, and (2) repetitive/restricted behaviors, including preoccupations with specific objects and repeated odd movements, such as hand flapping. About three-fourths of individuals with autism also meet criteria for intellectual disability or other serious cognitive deficits. Some are so verbally impaired that they are entirely mute. It is the latter individuals, those who are silent, for whom FC seemingly became a godsend.

Kanner's clinical descriptions were to foreshadow some later conceptualizations of the disorder. Although he offered no systematic evidence for this conjecture, Kanner contended that "although most of these children were at one time or another looked upon as feebleminded, they are all unquestionably endowed with good cognitive potentialities,"[5] a prescient passage to be cited approvingly by proponents of FC four decades later. He further observed that the minority of autistic children who could speak fluently displayed excellent vocabularies and intact, even superb, memory for events, visual patterns, and names.

Although acknowledging that autism is, in part, biologically influenced, Kanner viewed the condition mostly as a product of what later came to be called **refrigerator mothers:** mothers who are so cold, affectionless, and uncaring that their children escaped into private worlds of relative peace and comfort. Kanner reportedly opined that the parents—especially mothers—of children with autism had barely managed "to defrost enough to produce a child."[6] The view that autism is substantially of environmental origin was also popularized in the 1960s by child clinician Bruno Bettelheim, director of the Orthogenic School in Chicago.

A native of Austria and graduate of the University of Vienna, Bettelheim had been influenced by the thinking of one of Vienna's most famous citizens, Sigmund Freud. In Freud's view, psychopathology stemmed largely from derangements in parenting during the first few years of a child's development. In his poignant and emotionally provocative writings, including his widely read 1967 book *The Empty Fortress*, Bettelheim went much further than Kanner did in laying the blame for autism squarely on cold, rejecting parents. He asserted that autistic children were born neurologically normal, but became warped mentally by parents who failed to provide them with anything remotely approaching adequate affection. Bettelheim,[7] himself a Holocaust survivor, likened the parental environment of the autistic child to a concentration camp. Nevertheless, in some cases, he claimed, children with autism could be restored to healthy functioning by an intensive regimen of symbolic reparenting, in essence reversing the distant and uncaring treatment they had received early in life.

In the decades following World War II, the psychogenic views of Kanner and Bettelheim reigned supreme. They were passed on uncritically to a generation of psychology students, including the second author of this book (Scott), who read *The Empty Fortress* as part of a college course on mental illness. But by the late 1970s and early 1980s, studies conducted with twins had convincingly demonstrated the role of genetic factors in autism, and structural brain imaging studies suggested that autism is marked by obvious neurological abnormalities. For example, several research teams had demonstrated that individuals with autism often have abnormally large brains, probably reflecting a failure of adequate neuronal (brain cell) pruning in early development. Moreover, studies of family behavior had consistently failed to find the pronounced disturbances in early parenting posited by advocates of environmental models of autism.[8]

These and many other findings demonstrating abnormalities in the brains and biochemistry of individuals with autism[9] had dramatically shifted the scientific consensus away from the theoretical views of Kanner and Bettelheim. Psychosocial theories of autism were all but dead. Gone was the refrigerator mother concept; gone was the notion that autism stems from neglectful or emotionally abusive parents; and gone was the idea that lurking deep within the autistic individual is an intellectually intact mind. Yet these views were poised to make a startling comeback.

Origins of an Apparent Miracle

Perhaps more so than any psychological condition, autism has been remarkably fertile ground for fad and fringe treatments of various stripes. Table 2.1 is a partial list of treatments that have been widely used for autism. Some have been examined in controlled studies and found to be wanting, whereas others have been the subject of virtually no systematic research. Dozens of other scientifically unsupported interventions for autism have been tried with at best negligible success, and more often utter failure.

TABLE 2.1 A Partial List of Scientifically Unsupported Autism Treatments

acupuncture	Lupron (a drug that reduces levels of the hormones estradiol and testosterone)
art therapy	mineral solutions
chelation therapy (to remove lead, mercury, and other heavy metals from the body)	music therapy
dolphin-assisted therapy	"packing" (wrapping naked patients in cold, wet towels)
equine (horse)-assisted therapy	Pepcid (an antacid)
extended breast-feeding	secretin (a polypeptide hormone synthesized from the intestines of pigs)
gluten-free diets	sensory–motor integration training
herbal remedies	sheep stem cell injections
homeopathy	skull massage
hyperbaric oxygen treatment	trampoline therapy
hypnosis	

In modern-day France, some practitioners who treat older and more high-functioning individuals with autism have resorted to Freudian psychoanalysis, attempting to unearth hidden conflicts and repressed memories that presumably hold the key to the enigmatic symptoms of the condition. Of course, the mere fact that a seemingly never-ending succession of novel and unsupported treatments for autism have come and gone does not imply that another new intervention, such as FC, might not succeed.

Why has autism consistently been a magnet for novel and largely untested remedies? No one knows for certain, but we can offer six reasons. First and perhaps most important, parents of children with autism want desperately to "get through to" their children and to find some means of enabling them to succeed in life. One can hardly blame them. Understandably, many are willing to try almost anything that holds out even a slim hope of helping their children. In this regard, the allure of a quick and easy fix for a dreadfully intractable condition is difficult to resist. Only one method, applied behavior analysis (ABA), which systematically reinforces individuals with autism for adaptive behaviors, such as effective language use and appropriate social interactions, has consistently been shown in controlled studies to be helpful for autism.[10] Yet ABA is hardly a cure; the improvements it yields are often modest and incremental, and can take months to manifest themselves. Nor does ABA address what many experts regard as the core features of the condition, including profound deficits in social relatedness. Some parents who have tried ABA may become frustrated by the absence of dramatic improvements in their child's condition. As a consequence, they may turn elsewhere.

Second, as Binghamton University psychologist Raymond Romanczyk and his colleagues have pointed out, many of the symptoms of individuals with autism, such as odd movements or lack of interest in other people, frequently wax and wane over brief time intervals.[11] As a consequence, even entirely useless interventions may superficially seem to be effective if delivered when these symptoms happen to be manifesting themselves. This is especially likely to be the case given that practitioners often administer treatments when symptoms are at their worst—which is precisely when they are most likely to improve soon thereafter, a phenomenon that statisticians term **regression to the mean.** As the old saying goes, what goes up must come down, and the same holds for psychological symptoms.

Third, some people with autism, termed *savants* (meaning wise persons), display astonishing intellectual skills in one or a few circumscribed domains. Some know the exact batting averages of all Major League baseball players over the past 50 years; others can reproduce nearly any song on the piano after hearing it just once. One such individual, whom this book's second author (Scott) worked with for several months, was a "calendar calculator."[12] You could give him any day of any year, past or future, and he would cheerfully and immediately respond with the correct day of the week. The first time Scott met him, he asked Scott when he was born; when Scott replied, "December 23rd, 1960," the savant informed him that he had been born on a Friday (something Scott had not known). The existence of the savant syndrome, popularized in the 1988 film *Rain Man* starring Dustin Hoffman and Tom Cruise, may have fueled the perception that autism is a disorder marked by an intellectually intact mind trapped in a disordered body. In turn, this perception may have fostered an uncritical acceptance of interventions that purport to unveil autistic individuals' latent mental abilities.

Fourth, and in a related vein, what some authors have termed the *myth of unlimited potential* may have contributed to the popularity of certain autism interventions, including FC.[13] Much of popular psychology purveys the intuitively appealing notion that lying fallow within all of us is a vast untapped reservoir of intellectual ability. Many popular psychology sources still disseminate the outmoded claim that most of us use only 10% of our brains, and many films, such as the 2010 blockbuster movie *Inception*, have further perpetuated this notion (although *Inception*, oddly enough, informed viewers than we use only 20% of our brains). A great deal of scientific evidence, including data from brain imaging studies and investigations of people with brain damage, convincingly refutes the 10% belief, but it remains widespread among the general public. A 2010 survey by psychologists Christopher Chabris of Union College and Daniel Simons of the University of Illinois revealed that about two-thirds of American laypersons think that most people use only 10% of their brain capacity.[14] Perhaps as a consequence of this belief, many people may assume that individuals with autism will respond positively to certain interventions, such as FC, which can unlock their unrealized intellectual potential.

Fifth, the sway of psychoanalytic thinking continues to shape everyday psychology in potent ways. Although most orthodox Freudian concepts, such as the oral phase and Oedipus complex, have long been abandoned in the mainstream scientific community, they remain pervasive in much of popular psychology. Most of the American public continues to embrace some influential Freudian ideas, such as the notion that all mental illnesses can be traced to repressed trauma in childhood.[15] Content analyses also demonstrate that in movies and cartoons, psychotherapy is still typically depicted as classical psycho-analysis, with clients reclining on a couch and retracing their painful childhood memories.[16] Moreover, the plots of innumer-able Hollywood films, such as *Good Will Hunting* and *Mystic River*, embody what we might term the *abuse narrative*. This now-familiar story line involves a troubled individual who re-covers long-forgotten memories of childhood abuse, or comes to grips emotionally with such abuse, followed by an intense emotional release (the catharsis) and dramatic psychological improvement. The remarkable persistence of Freudian views, especially those emphasizing the causal role of early traumatic events, may account for the popular appeal of autism interven-tions designed to ameliorate the influence of these events.

Sixth, in contrast to most conditions often associated with marked intellectual impairment, such as Down, Turner's, and fetal alcohol syndromes, autism is not associated with any ob-vious facial dysmorphic features. Indeed, many if not most individuals with autism look physically normal. This normal appearance may lead some inadequately trained practitioners to assume that individuals with the condition must also be, deep down, psychologically normal as well.[17]

In view of all these considerations, it should come as little surprise that FC met with a receptive audience when it arrived on the scene. It was premised on the seductive idea that people with autism are cognitively normal, not intellectually impaired, and it appeared to solve the profound communicative and so-cial deficits of autism in one fell swoop. It also implied that con-necting with autistic children emotionally was only a keystroke away. In many ways, FC was just what the doctor ordered—or, more accurately, precisely what our wishes wanted.

The Origin and Spread of Facilitated Communication

Facilitated communication traces its roots to St. Nicholas Hospital, an institution for children and adults with severe multiple intellectual and physical disabilities in Melbourne, Australia. There, in 1977, a teacher and disability rights advocate named Rosemary Crossley claimed to have hit upon a novel technique for extracting communications from people who were nonverbal and assumed to be cognitively impaired. Having worked extensively with these people, Crossley had a suspicion that they were far more intelligent than others had given them credit for. Crossley termed her technique facilitated communication training (or facilitated communication for short), and administered it primarily to individuals with severe physical disabilities that precluded speech, such as cerebral palsy.[18]

Crossley's reported findings were remarkable. After using her method with 12 individuals suffering from severe physical and mental impairments, she concluded that despite widespread beliefs that they were cognitively impaired, all of them were of at least normal intelligence. All of them, she claimed, could now communicate effectively despite years of silence. St. Nicholas Hospital questioned Crossley's findings and conclusions, as did a number of autism experts in Australia, but she boldly persevered. Crossley refused demands for independent testing of her claims, largely on the grounds that because people with severe impairments do not appreciate having their intellectual abilities questioned, any negative results would be essentially meaningless. As you may recall from the previous chapter, Wilhelm von Osten had proposed a similar explanation when he implied that any negative results from Clever Hans were meaningless because the horse did not appreciate having to answer questions from people who were less intelligent than he was. In 1986 Crossley founded the Dignity, Education, Advocacy, Language (DEAL) Centre, an institute in Melbourne dedicated to helping people with serious speech disabilities find ways to communicate. Soon, FC flourished in a number of local school districts in Australia.

Still, at this point, FC was largely unknown in the United States or elsewhere. That was not to be for long. In 1989 Douglas Biklen, a sociologist and professor of special education at Syracuse University in upstate New York, traveled to Australia to observe Crossley's methods and reported achievements. Biklen was profoundly impressed by what he saw, and he immediately came to regard facilitated communication as a landmark discovery. He returned to America determined to spread the word. Crossley had intended facilitated communication to be used primarily for children with obvious physical disabilities, such as cerebral palsy, or with well-established genetic disorders associated with intellectual disability, such as Down syndrome or phenylketonuria (PKU). In contrast, Biklen envisioned the method as having far more sweeping clinical applications.[19] Upon returning to Syracuse, he experimented with the use of FC to enable communication among nonverbal children with autism, and reported astounding results.

Biklen formally unveiled the startling news in a 1990 article in the prestigious *Harvard Educational Review*, which granted facilitated communication an imprimatur of scientific respectability,[20] just as the Hans Commission had lent credibility to Wilhelm von Osten and Clever Hans a century earlier. Several other articles in high-profile journals by Biklen and his collaborators, including Donald Cardinal at Chapman University in

The signal from Mr. von Osten to Clever Hans began innocently when the old schoolmaster knelt on the ground to lift the horse's hoof as he pronounced the number "one." After Hans had tapped the correct number, von Osten would look up and reward Hans with some bread or a piece of carrot. (Krall, Karl. *Denkende Tiere: Beitrage zur Tierseelenkunde auf Grund eigener Versuche.* Leipzig: Engelmann, 1912, p. 14)

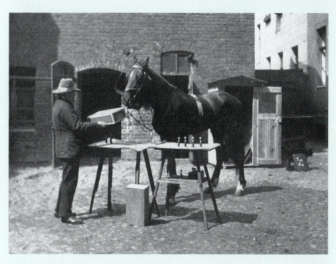

In order to teach the concept of addition to Clever Hans, von Osten emphasized the word "and" just as he revealed more pegs. He did not realize that bending forward to better observe Clever Hans's hoof had become the signal that the always hungry horse was waiting for. (Krall, Karl. *Denkende Tiere: Beitrage zur Tierseelenkunde auf Grund eigener Versuche.* Leipzig: Engelmann, 1912, p. 16)

Children would sometimes make fun of the old bachelor and his peculiar ways. Their attitudes changed when high-ranking military authorities, social dignitaries, and famous scientists began visiting their humble courtyard. Neighbors verified to the press that Mr. von Osten had educated Clever Hans every day in the courtyard. (Krall, Karl. *Denkende Tiere: Beitrage zur Tierseelenkunde auf Grund eigener Versuche.* Leipzig: Engelmann, 1912, p. 428)

Notice the angle of Mr. von Osten's head as Clever Hans paws the ground. A slight head movement forward would start Hans tapping; a slight lifting up would signal Hans to stop tapping. The signal was difficult to detect because everyone naturally leaned forward to observe Clever Hans's hoof and then leaned back in admiration when he arrived at the proper number. (Krall, Karl. *Denkende Tiere: Beitrage zur Tierseelenkunde auf Grund eigener Versuche.* Leipzig: Engelmann, 1912, p. 22)

Many people came to believe in Clever Hans after the expert horseman, retired General Zobel (second from right), gave his public endorsement. When we are uncertain about what to believe, we often look to authority figures for guidance. (Krall, Karl. *Denkende Tiere: Beitrage zur Tierseelenkunde auf Grund eigener Versuche.* Leipzig: Engelmann, 1912, p. 68)

Clever Hans's abilities declined when he was made to wear these large blinkers, which limited his ability to see Mr. von Osten. The results of this experiment initially convinced von Osten that he was accidentally signaling his horse, but by the next morning he had changed his mind again. (Krall, Karl. *Denkende Tiere: Beitrage zur Tierseelenkunde auf Grund eigener Versuche.* Leipzig: Engelmann, 1912, p. 6)

This headline demonstrates how the media often misrepresent psychological findings as more dramatic than they really are. The commission never decided that Clever Hans was able to reason. (The New York Times, 1904)

"CLEVER HANS" AGAIN.

Expert Commission Decides That the Horse Actually Reasons.

From The London Standard.

BERLIN, Sept. 13.—The remarkable horse called "Clever Hans" has just been examined by a special commission of experts, in order that a decision might be arrived at whether it is a horse possessed of extraordinary brain power or merely, like many others of its tribe, peculiarly adapted to learning tricks from patient trainers. The commission consisted of the well-known circus proprietor, Herr Paul Busch; Count Otto zu Castell Ruedenhausen, a retired army Captain; Dr. Grabow, a retired schoolmaster; Dr. Ludwig Heck, Director of the Berlin Zoological Gardens; Major von Keller, Major. Gen. Koering, Dr. Miessner, a veterinary surgeon; Prof. Nagel of the Physiological Institute of the University of Berlin, and several other prominent men.

The commission has issued a statement declaring that it is of opinion that there is no trickery whatever in the performances of the horse, and that the methods employed by the owner, Herr von Osten, in teaching Hans differ essentially from those used by trainers, and correspond with those used in teaching children in elementary schools. They hold that the methods employed have in principle nothing whatever to do with "training" in the accepted sense of the word, and are worthy of scientific examination. The report of these gentlemen is interesting, for Herr von Osten had tried in vain to persuade scientific men to take the case of "Clever Hans" seriously. Herr Busch, of circus fame, who was one of the commission, had openly admitted beforehand that he was extremely skeptical about the matter, and believed that the horse had been taught merely to learn a few clever tricks just like other well-known circus horses. Now, however, he admits that he was mistaken.

The New York Times

Published: October 2, 1904
Copyright © The New York Times

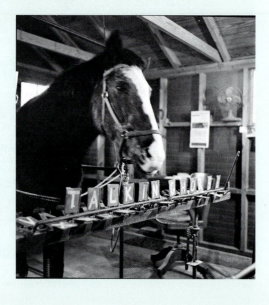

Beautiful Jim Key (top) was an American wonder horse with his own pavilion at the 1904 St. Louis World's Fair. A few years later, Lady Wonder from Virginia (right) joined the list of equine sensations with supposed psychic powers. (Top: Courtesy of the Tennessee State Library and Archives, Beautiful Jim Key Collection; right: Photo by Hank Walker/The LIFE Picture Collection/Getty Images)

Mr. von Osten lived alone in one of the fifth floor apartments overlooking the courtyard and Clever Hans's stall. Clever Hans was to be the crowning achievement of his life. (Krall, Karl. *Denkende Tiere: Beitrage zur Tierseelenkunde auf Grund eigener Versuche.* Leipzig: Engelmann, 1912)

When Germany's most famous scientist Professor C. G. Schillings endorsed Clever Hans, he influenced other scientists as well as the general public to believe that Clever Hans really could think like a human. Schillings arrived as a skeptic, became a believer, and then returned to his scientifically driven skepticism. (Image from *With flashlight and rifle, a record of hunting adventures and of studies in wildlife in Equatorial East-Africa* (1906) by Carl Georg Schillings)

Julian and Thal Wendrow talk to the *Detroit Free Press* about their ordeal in Bloomfield Hills, Mich., on Feb. 8, 2011. (SUSAN TUSA/MCT/ Newscom)

Illustration depicting facilitated communication. (©Pat Linse, Skeptic Magazine)

Document from police report on Aislinn's facilitated allegation of sexual abuse against her father. Note that the line for "Alternative Hypothesis" is left blank.

The Johns Hopkins University psychiatrist Leo Kanner, who in 1943 was the first scholar to systematically describe the core features of autism. (Science Source)

Bruno Bettelheim, who popularized the notion that autism is a condition of environmental etiology, produced by cold and uncaring parents. (© Bettmann/CORBIS)

Ouija board, along with a planchette. Most scientists believe that facilitated communication and the Ouija board both play on people's expectations: the ideomotor effect. (Ellen Denuto/Getty Images)

An 1863 drawing of a person engaged in automatic writing. He is surrounded by spirits, including the devil, who are supposedly controlling his arm and hand movements. (Sophia Elizabeth Frend De Morgan, Augustus De Morgan, *From Matter to Spirit, The Result of Ten Years' Experience in Spirit Manifestations. Intended as a Guide to Enquirers*, Pub. Longman, Green, Longman, Roberts, & Green, 1863.)

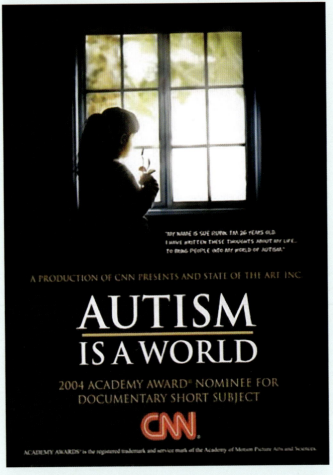

"MY NAME IS SUE RUBIN. I'M 26 YEARS OLD. I HAVE WRITTEN THESE THOUGHTS ABOUT MY LIFE... TO BRING PEOPLE INTO MY WORLD OF AUTISM."

A PRODUCTION OF CNN PRESENTS AND STATE OF THE ART INC.

AUTISM
IS A WORLD

2004 ACADEMY AWARD® NOMINEE FOR
DOCUMENTARY SHORT SUBJECT

CNN.

ACADEMY AWARDS® is the registered trademark and service mark of the Academy of Motion Picture Arts and Sciences.

Autism Is a World, a film about Sue Rubin, a young woman with autism, was narrated by actor Julianna Margulies. It was nominated for an Academy Award in 2004 for Best Documentary Short Subject. It portrayed FC as a breakthrough intervention for autism. What will we do when the scientific evidence clearly contradicts something we want to believe? (CNN)

Belgian car accident victim Rom Houben using facilitated communication. (Tony Van Galen/ Abaca/Newscom)

Janyce Boynton is now a successful artist and designer in Maine. Formerly a facilitator, she has become a public critic of the technique. (Courtesy Janyce Boynton, Courtesy Maine Women's Fund)

The YouTube video of Potato shows how the dog's owner lifts his head to stop Potato's barking at the correct number. It is difficult to notice the signal, especially if you already believe in Potato's abilities. (CCTV)

Crowds of tourists ooh, aah, and spend lots of money as they observe elephants paint surprisingly beautiful works of art. But notice that the handler is looking intently at the painting and using his hand on the elephant's ear to signal the elephant what to do next. It is an impressive trick in its own right, but does not demonstrate visual creativity by these elephants. Check it out at http://tinyurl.com/byswd7. (© epa european pressphoto agency b.v. / Alamy)

We want to believe in the abilities of drug-sniffing dogs but even these super-sniffers can be influenced by cues from their handlers. Like Mr. von Osten with Clever Hans, the dogs' handlers are probably unaware that they may be signaling their dogs. (Billy Hustace/Getty Images)

Intuition is wrong about the program Scared Straight. It seems like it should work; we want it to work; and we hope that it works. Unfortunately, many studies have demonstrated that it is more likely to do harm than good. (© Rose Palmisano/The Orange County Register/ZUMAPRESS.com)

$185 million in sales demonstrate how well skillful marketers understand the Clever Hans effect. Parents want to believe in the *Your Baby Can Read* videos and are willing to pay hard-earned money for a product with dubious benefits. (Courtesy Lori Granieri)

California, soon followed. Biklen's rationale for using facilitated communication with autism was revolutionary but straightforward. According to Biklen, virtually all experts had been fundamentally mistaken about the nature of autism. This condition, he maintained, is fundamentally a motor disorder—a disorder of movement—not a mental disorder, as had long been believed. Biklen may well have been influenced by the writings of Kanner, who conjectured that most or all children with autism are intelligent, even though they cannot display their cognitive abilities in everyday behavior.

According to Biklen, the person with autism is cognitively intact, but suffers from an underlying condition that he termed **developmental dyspraxia.** This subtle but pervasive motor abnormality not only prevents many individuals with autism from speaking (in milder cases, it diminishes their ability to speak fluently), but it also prevents them from "typing" on their own, justifying the need for a facilitator to stabilize their arm and hand movements. Once this abnormality in movement is corrected, argued Biklen,[21] the underlying intelligence of people with autism can emerge triumphantly from its prison of silence.

Biklen proved to be an articulate and persuasive spokesperson, and his interpersonal skills and energy played no small part in fueling facilitated communication's popularity. Owing in no small measure to his tireless efforts and those of his colleagues, as well as to the hope that their work inspired in countless parents and teachers, FC spread like wildfire throughout the autism community. Although precise numbers are hard to come by, hundreds of school districts in the United States began to use the technique in the years following its introduction to America, and conferences and weekend workshops designed to train educators in the technique proliferated. Many of these conferences attracted hundreds of enthusiastic participants, and some featured live facilitated "presentations" by people with autism and other developmental disabilities. Scores of school districts not only changed fundamentally their methods of teaching children with autism, but also altered their very understanding of what the disorder was.

Many children and adolescents with autism who were previously presumed to be mentally retarded were now mainstreamed into regular classes where they accomplished coursework with the aid of FC. Some school psychologists and other mental health professionals began administering intelligence tests under FC conditions, resulting in increases of dozens of points in estimated IQ. In a number of cases, children diagnosed previously as mentally retarded were reclassified as of normal intelligence. Some colleges and universities even began offering courses that allowed students to receive certification in FC.[22] In 1992 Biklen opened the Facilitated Communication Institute at Syracuse University, which promoted the use of FC through brochures, newsletters, workshops, and later, Internet postings.

Biklen wrote an article in the *New York Times Magazine* in 1991, touting the method as a remarkable innovation in autism treatment. The popular media took notice. The communication networks were far more sophisticated than they had been in 1904 when Clever Hans's story was capturing international headlines, but the journalism was scarcely more critical. Soon dozens of major newspapers and magazines published enthusiastic stories on FC, many without a hint that the method had yet to be subjected to careful scientific scrutiny. *CBS News* ran an equally laudatory story concerning FC on television. In 1992 ABC's *Primetime Live* television show featured a segment on

FC, with host Diane Sawyer introducing the show by telling viewers that "for decades, autism has been a dark mystery, a disorder that seems to turn children in on themselves, against the world. Tonight, however, you are going to see something that has changed that. Call it a miracle. Call it an awakening."[23]

It was not just the media and practitioners who became believers; parents and other loved ones did so as well. One of them, much as Professor Schillings had done for Clever Hans and Maurice Maeterlinck had done for Mohammed, lent facilitated communication a particular cachet of scientific respectability. Arthur Schawlow, who had received the Nobel Prize in Physics in 1981, was the father of an autistic son. Asked in a 1993 documentary what more evidence he needed to become persuaded of FC's effectiveness, Schawlow responded, "I don't need any more validation. My son has given me a lot of information, much of which I didn't know."[24] Schawlow's unqualified endorsement was another boost to the credibility of FC, as it demonstrated that unquestionably brilliant individuals could become convinced of the technique's effectiveness.

FC was more than a breakthrough for autism; it was a genuine paradigm shift. It seemed not only to unlock the hidden communicative capacities presumably harbored by individuals with autism, but also to overturn the overwhelming scientific consensus regarding this condition. Suddenly, everything that autism experts had believed to be settled knowledge, and everything they had taught their students, were wrong. Autism, it now appeared, was not a mental disorder after all. Nor were people with the condition cognitively impaired in any fundamental way. Instead, autism was at its core a disorder of movement that could be treated using nothing more than the physical support of a caring and patient assistant. Mental health professionals had long become accustomed to rolling their eyes at the hackneyed phrase "miracle cure," as time and again purported overnight cures had fizzled before their eyes. Yet FC was the exception that proved the rule, or so it seemed. It offered every indication of being the real thing.

The Great Unraveling

The wheels of science often turn slowly. Although science is inherently a self-correcting enterprise, misguided scientific ideas commonly persist for years, even decades, before they are weeded out by the safeguards of research methodology. It took a few decades, for example, for the once popular idea that autism is caused by refrigerator parents to be convincingly debunked by the research community. Yet, on rare occasions, the wheels of science spin rapidly, especially when sensational claims are advanced and people's livelihoods are at stake.

Not long after FC was introduced, a cadre of well-established researchers in the autism community demanded that its claims be put to controlled experimental tests. Many FC proponents were bewildered by this insistence, as it struck them as self-evident that the technique worked. After all, they had seen the typing with their own eyes, and it was unclear to them what additional evidence was required. Yet, by their very nature, scientists tend to be a skeptical bunch, and many seasoned autism researchers and clinicians, including James Mulick of The Ohio State University, John Jacobson in Schenectady, New York, Howard Shane of Boston's Children's Hospital, Raymond Romanczyk of Binghamton University, and Raymond

Miltenberger, then at North Dakota State University, were dubious of what they had seen and heard about facilitated communication. Here's why.

From the outset, a number of salient facts about FC struck autism experts as exceedingly peculiar. First, videotapes of many children engaged in FC, even with experienced assistants, demonstrated that the children's eyes were not consistently looking at the keys as they typed. Some were glancing away entirely. How, critics wondered, could children be typing without looking at the keys? Studies showed that even experienced typists could not pull off that feat without first positioning their hands,[25] so it seemed implausible that children with severe or profound intellectual disability could manage to do it.

Second, experts wondered where individuals with severe autism could have acquired their immense hidden knowledge about the world. Many of these people were previously unable to read anything complicated. In some cases, they displayed no evidence of being able to read at all before working with an FC facilitator. Virtually all of them had shown scant interest in books or other written material. Nor did most children with autism seem to pay much attention to adult conversations about mundane topics, much less lofty intellectual matters.

Third, using FC, most people with autism displayed advanced knowledge that seemed to go far beyond their years and even the most generous estimates of their intellectual capacities. Even though the majority were unable to point to the correct letter (such as *A*) when given the choice between two letters (such as *A* and *B*), many wrote at great length and in eloquent terms of their love for their parents and their career dreams. One individual asked for a change in his medication after supposedly reading a research article in the *New England Journal of Medicine*; another child previously estimated by a psychologist as having an IQ of 19 (in the profoundly retarded range) typed the statement "I am not retarded. I am intelligent" without any spelling errors. At a major conference on FC, one person with autism, Jeff Powell, typed the following impassioned defense of Doug Biklen—with the aid of an FC facilitator:

> Regarding the recent controversy about facilitated communication, we are extremely angry about the well-to-do critics who are giving Doug a disheartening review. We are the ones saying the words and we are questioning the expertise of you and your compassion for autistic students. And please encourage us and Doug to be able to become a part of your world and get the hell out of our world.[26]

FC also enabled people with autism to write poetry, some of which displayed impressive depth and maturity. One 29-year-old man from Madison, Wisconsin, diagnosed with autism, used FC to write a poem entitled "Listen to My Heart." The poem began:

> *Please listen to my heart*
> *Please forgive these clumsy words*
> *Just hear me from my open heart to yours*
> *The language of my heart speaks eloquently*
> *While my fingers grapple for the letters one at atime*
> *(sic).*
> *My mouth has nothing to say.*

Heart language remembers the beginning
And forsees (sic) the end
It holds my whole life in one single glance
And tries to convey everything at once.

Words on the other hand
Break it all up into
a thousand tiny pieces
Which never go back together again.[27]

Such words are moving, to be sure. But are they really plausible? The lives led by many people with autism provide few opportunities to acquire complex language and a sophisticated understanding of metaphors. None of these vexing questions demonstrated that facilitated communication was illegitimate, of course. For one thing, these isolated examples could be atypical, or they might reflect misuses or abuses of the technique. Good scientists are well aware of the principle of *abusus non tollit usum*: the abuse or misuse of a claim doesn't invalidate it. Moreover, some accepted truths in science occasionally turn out to be flat-out wrong. For decades, German scientist Alfred Wegener's theory of continental drift, introduced in 1912, was roundly ridiculed by fellow researchers.[28] Given what they then knew about geography and seismology, the notion of moving continents struck most of them as laughable. Yet, as we now know, Wegener was ultimately vindicated by findings regarding plate tectonics, and his theory is now universally accepted by earth scientists. Perhaps FC would turn out to be a similar example of a revolutionary but correct idea that was initially resisted by the scientific community merely because it ran counter to prevailing orthodoxy.

Even so, the puzzling facts regarding facilitated communication could not be readily dismissed. At the very least, they raised significant red flags in the minds of even the most open-minded of autism researchers. As sociologist Marcello Truzzi and, later, astronomer and science writer Carl Sagan reminded us, extraordinary claims require extraordinary evidence. Putting it a bit differently, assertions that fly in the face of just about everything we know—well, those assertions *might* be right—but we need especially convincing evidence before accepting them. Novelty is not necessarily progress. In the case of FC, the claims were certainly extraordinary, but the evidence—compelling on its surface—came exclusively from testimonials and anecdotal observations.

Psychological interventions based on anecdotes have at best a mixed track record. A handful have been disastrous. To take merely one of many examples, hundreds of surgeons in the 1940s and 1950s concluded that prefrontal lobotomy was effective for alleviating the symptoms of schizophrenia and other serious mental disorders. They justified this radical procedure based largely on informal observations of patient improvement following the operation.[29] As in the case of von Osten and Clever Hans, they fell prey to naive realism, assuming that "seeing is believing." Indeed, the principal pioneer of prefrontal lobotomy, Portuguese neurosurgeon Egas Moniz, won the Nobel Prize for its application to psychopathology in 1949. It was only later—in the United States alone, about 50,000 surgeries too late—that controlled research demonstrated the procedure to be ineffective and, worse, associated with a host of disastrous side effects. The sordid history of lobotomy[30] reminds us that psychologists dare not assume that FC (or any other intervention) is effective without rigorous controlled tests.

Indeed, beginning in the early 1990s, researchers applied two major laboratory tests to FC. In some ways, these tests were similar in design to Oskar Pfungst's "crucial" tests on Clever Hans. Recall that Pfungst tested the horse when the questioner, typically von Osten, was either "with knowledge" or "without knowledge" of the correct answer. In the case of FC, a crucial experiment required keeping facilitators "blind" (without knowledge) of the information available to the person with autism.

As critics had observed, the standard procedure used by Biklen and other FC to validate this technique was flawed, because the facilitator was typically aware of the correct answers to the questions posed to the child. The only proper way to evaluate FC, they noted, is to ensure that the facilitator does not have access to the same information provided to the child. As psychological scientists have long known, blinded designs (those without knowledge) are essential safeguards against mind bugs, especially confirmation bias. Without these designs, we can easily draw erroneous conclusions about whether a method works, because our expectations can influence what we find and what we observe.

The first test of facilitated communication, called a *message passing* procedure, was both simple and realistic. It was so straightforward, in fact, that in retrospect it is surprising that FC advocates had not thought of it themselves. In a message passing test, the researcher hands the autistic individual a specific object, such as a set of keys, with the facilitator out of the room. The keys are then removed from sight, and the facilitator returns. The researcher then asks the autistic individual to type the name of the object with the aid of the facilitator. If the autistic individual genuinely possesses knowledge, he or she should be able—with the facilitator's help—to use one or more fingers to type "keys." But if the person cannot type "keys," it indicates that facilitated communication "works" only when the facilitator possesses knowledge of the object.

The second crucial test of FC was a bit more complicated, but also more elegant. In this design, the facilitator and child are seated in adjoining cubicles, but with an opening between them to permit hand-to-hand contact on a keyboard placed before the child. In front of them is a wall on which pictures can be displayed; because child and facilitator are in different cubicles, they can see only the picture shown to them, not the picture shown to their partner. On some trials, facilitator and child are shown the same image. For example, in some cases, both might be shown a photograph of a hamburger. But on other trials, the "test" trials, facilitator and child see different images; for example, one might view a photograph of a dog, the other a photograph of a cat. Following each trial, the experimenters ask the child, with the aid of the facilitator, to type what he or she saw. The crucial question is this: On the test trials, will the words typed correspond to the images seen by the child, as FC proponents would predict, or by the facilitator? Again, if the word typed was consistently the word seen by facilitators, it would strongly suggest that the communication originated from them, not the individuals with autism.[31]

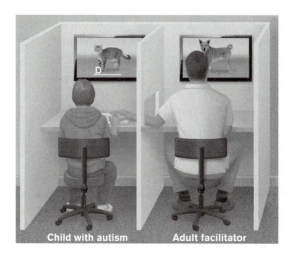

Crucial experimental test for facilitated communication.

The results of both crucial experiments stunned the world of FC. The studies came from multiple independent laboratories around the country, yet they were remarkably consistent, and they appeared in prestigious, peer-reviewed scientific journals. In carefully controlled published trials, children with autism were unable to produce *any* correct responses in the test trials.[32]

The consensus of the scientific community became more assertive as multiple well-controlled studies appeared in the early 1990s, virtually all with uniformly negative results. These investigations exemplified science as its best, as they convincingly ruled out the rival hypothesis that the seeming success of FC was due to the innermost thoughts of individuals with autism. The authors of a 1995 review published in *American Psychologist*, the American Psychological Association's flagship journal, concluded that "controlled research using single and double-blind procedures in laboratory and natural settings with clinical populations with which FC (facilitated communication) is used have determined that . . . people with disabilities [are] unable to respond accurately to label or describe stimuli unseen by their assistants."[33] By 1999 there were 18 published well-controlled trials of FC, with 183 total opportunities for children with autism to provide correct responses. The box score across these 18 studies was a startling 0 out of 183.[34]

Later, a handful of trials with favorable results emerged in a few published studies, but these results were quickly rebutted by behavioral scientists. Why? In these studies facilitators had access to knowledge about the stimulus materials, making it logically impossible to rule out the rival hypothesis of inadvertent facilitator influence. As the late University of Minnesota clinical psychologist Paul Meehl noted in 1967,[35] a handy rule of thumb in science is that when effects are genuine, they should become larger in magnitude when more rigorous experimental controls are imposed. Yet, in FC, as in the case of Clever Hans, we witnessed the opposite. Effects emerged only when experimental controls were absent or sloppy, and disappeared when they were stringent.

In science, especially psychological science, it is exceedingly rare to find instances of unanimously negative results across scores of independent studies. Yet despite multiple tests by different investigative teams, FC had failed—and failed spectacularly. The evidence, incredible as it seemed, pointed overwhelmingly to unintentional control of the autistic individuals' arm and hand movements by facilitators. The facilitators, it seemed, were doing the typing themselves without realizing it.[36] What had been going on?

The answer, oddly enough, comes in part from scientific work testing spiritualism. In essence, the FC keyboard appears to be little more than a modern version of the Ouija board. The board is familiar to devotees of the supernatural and to children and adults alike, who find it an enjoyable parlor game. It is a flat board onto which are printed the letters of the alphabet, numbers from 0 to 9, and several words (such as "yes," "no," and "goodbye"). The board comes with a planchette, a triangular device fitted with small wheels or felt pads that enable users to roll or slide it to various sectors of the board. Invented and first marketed in 1890 by an American businessman, the Ouija board was used for entertainment until about two decades later, when spiritual mediums—psychics who claimed to be able to communicate with the afterworld—began to use it in an attempt to contact the dead. This practice became more prevalent during and after World War I, when psychics enjoyed a lucrative business helping grieving families feel connected to their loved ones, especially those who had been killed in the war.[37] Ouija participants typically ask a question of a deceased person ("Are you in heaven now?"), place their fingers on the planchette, watch it move, and observe where it ends up. Often, the planchette lands on an answer that seems to make sense, or that can at least be interpreted as meaningful in hindsight. The players in the game of Ouija feel as if the planchette is moving on its own, although it is of course actually being guided by their unconscious intentions.

Long before FC appeared on the scene, psychologists had known that people's thoughts can influence their actions without their knowledge, a phenomenon they termed the **ideomotor effect,** a term that captures the fact that our ideas can affect our movements.[38] For centuries, mystics had engaged in a procedure called *automatic writing:* After entering a trance, they began writing gibberish that supposedly granted them privileged access to their unconscious thoughts and feelings. In some cases, automatic writers believed that their movements were being controlled by demons or other spirits. Automatic writing and a parallel phenomenon that we might call *automatic talking* enjoyed a resurgence in the 1970s with the popularity of *channeling,* in which a person claims to be invaded by the spirit of a deceased individual who speaks and/or writes through the *channeler.* Like Ouija board players, automatic writers harbor the powerful subjective conviction that their actions are being willed by an external force. Another famous illustration of the ideomotor effect is the *Chevreul pendulum* (named after a French chemist who was a skeptic of paranormal claims), which can be constructed easily at home using nothing more than a string and a small weight appended to the bottom of it. Tell a friend holding the pendulum that it is slowly beginning to move clockwise (or counterclockwise), and more often than not, it will.[39]

What makes the ideomotor effect especially striking is that the "victims" of the illusion are almost always oblivious to its existence, insisting that they are not moving anything. As a consequence, they may become convinced that the movements are generated by something outside of them—an invisible force or, in the case of the Ouija board, a disembodied spirit from another dimension.

The ideomotor effect is almost certainly a prime culprit in the apparent effectiveness of FC. Much like von Osten and the "experts" who addressed questions to Clever Hans, FC facilitators are not consciously deceiving anyone. They sincerely believe that they are not controlling their partner's arm and hand movements, even though they are. In recognition of the striking historical parallels, some scientists began to refer to the FC debacle as the tale of "Clever Hands."[40] In both cases, researchers noted, the hapless participants of the illusion were responding to subtle cues without their knowledge.

The ideomotor effect, though, is only part of the explanation for facilitated communication. What Harvard psychologist B. F. Skinner termed **shaping by successive approximations** (or **shaping** for short) almost certainly plays a key role. Over time, child and facilitator unknowingly and mutually reinforce one another's slight hand movements, just as Clever Hans and von Osten had reinforced each other's actions. The facilitator gradually becomes accustomed to the child's hand movements, and learns which movements become reinforced with "correct" answers—those that correspond to what the facilitator wants to see. The child, in turn, gradually learns to follow the gentle lead of the facilitator, allowing her or his hands to be guided by the facilitator's barely visible arm motions.

Naïve realism almost surely plays a part, too, just as it did in the case of Clever Hans. Facilitators witness the dramatic effects of the technique with their own eyes, and they understandably find it difficult to deny the obvious evidence of their perceptions. Yet we also discovered in Chapter 1 that sometimes believing is seeing, rather than vice versa. The facilitators trying to help people with developmental disabilities to communicate see only what they want to see, namely, that FC appears to work. There is no ill will; the self-deception is sincere. The illusion of facilitated communication is further fueled by confirmation bias, the tendency—whether conscious or unconscious—to attend only to evidence that confirms what we believe. Similar to what von Osten did when questioning Clever Hans, FC aides ask certain questions and usually receive the answers they are hoping and expecting to receive, largely because they themselves are formulating the responses.

Compounding the error, FC practitioners may exercise selective judgments about the kinds of responses a child provides. Answers that are well formulated and articulate are interpreted as reflections of the nonverbal person's hidden intelligence, whereas answers that are incoherent or meaningless can easily be sloughed off as the products of fatigue, poor motivation, distraction, or resistance to being tested. In still other cases, ambiguous answers can be interpreted in light of one's desires and expectations. One girl with autism, featured in a 1993 documentary,[41] enjoyed seeing her father wiggle his nose. One day, upon arriving home, she looked for her father to no avail, and typed "I-M-S-N-O-S" with the aid of her facilitator. The mother immediately interpreted the message as meaning "I miss nose."

Cognitive dissonance also plays a role, just as it did in the case of von Osten and Clever Hans's other advocates. Recall that cognitive dissonance is the tendency to experience mental tension when two or more of our thoughts come into conflict. When we experience such dissonance, we're motivated to reduce it, often by persuading ourselves that the evidence underlying one of these thoughts is erroneous. In the case of FC, most facilitators may resolve their dissonance simply by persuading themselves that they are right, and that the scientific studies are wrong.

As the uniformly negative evidence against FC mounted in the early and mid-1990s, its proponents began to resort to a host of post-hoc hypotheses to explain away the disappointing findings—in much the same way that Clever Hans's errors were blamed on fatigue, stubbornness, not-being-in-the-mood, and other increasingly far-fetched explanations. Some FC advocates maintained, for example, that the experimental tests were invalid because they placed children with autism in a "confrontational" or "adversarial" situation in which they felt pressured to perform. Donald Cardinal, a professor of education at Chapman University (and as noted earlier, a collaborator of Biklen's), contended that formal tests of FC were too stressful for childhood participants, rendering negative results difficult or impossible to interpret. Other FC advocates charged that because the controlled trials took place in novel environments or involved unfamiliar equipment, they yielded suboptimal performances. Still others argued that if participants only had more time to respond, they surely would have produced a few correct answers.

The obvious problem with these post-hoc arguments, however, is that many of the same children who had failed formal, controlled tests of FC had earlier been able to facilitate at professional conferences in front of video cameras and hundreds of transfixed onlookers. Many of these children had also performed well on intelligence tests and passed high-pressure examinations in their courses, or readily facilitated in other new surroundings, typing out detailed answers to complicated questions with minimal delay. The critics of the controlled studies also ignored the fact that in most published research, children were paired with facilitators to whom they were accustomed and were reinforced with their favorite goodies for correct answers.

The sad case of Aislinn Wendrow exemplifies this overuse of post-hoc arguments. There were obvious telltale signs that the sentences purportedly emanating from Aislinn were actually originating from her facilitator, but believers in the technique turned a blind eye to them. For example, Aislinn could not correctly spell the name of her brother Ian, but she could correctly spell the name of Scarsella's brother. Some of Aislinn's communications discussed her religious views; yet these messages mentioned themes from Christianity, which was Scarsella's religion—not Judaism, which was the Wendrows'. Again, confirmation bias and cognitive dissonance probably conspired to make facilitated communication advocates ignore or reinterpret evidence that contradicted their views.

More broadly, all these valiant defenses neglected an obvious counterargument. In principle, these explanations might partly account for why the performance of children in these studies was less than perfect, or why children committed more errors in controlled tests than they did in their natural environments. Yet none of these post-hoc hypotheses could account for why, in well-controlled trials, children who could compose lengthy poems or multiple-page essays using FC were suddenly unable to produce any correct answers to the simplest of questions.

The devastating research findings were not the only death knell for FC's now embattled reputation in the scientific community. There also was the damning issue of sexual abuse allegations. The Wendrows, Storches, Wheatons, and dozens of other families had endured horrific and humiliating accusations of abuse, and in some cases separation from their families and jail time, on the basis of nothing more than facilitated accusations of abuse. The substantial majority of these allegations were never corroborated, and even in the cases in which they were, it was unclear whether facilitators might have had indirect access to information about the parents that tipped them off to the abuse.

The tragic case of the Wendrows that opened this chapter can hardly be said to have a "happy" ending. But at least it came to a satisfactory resolution in the eyes of the Wendrows. In the courtroom, Howard Shane, a psychologist at Boston Children's Hospital and a noted critic of FC, persuaded the judge, Marc Barron, to allow Aislinn to answer a series of questions while her facilitator, Cynthia Scarsella, stepped outside of the courtroom. With Julian Wendrow, still imprisoned and dressed in an orange jumpsuit, watching from the back of the courtroom, Aislinn attempted to answer a series of 18 questions about herself and her family. In each case, attorneys asked Aislinn a simple question with Scarsella absent, and then Scarsella reentered the courtroom to facilitate Aislinn's responses.

"What color is your sweater?" Aislinn was asked.

Her facilitated response: "JIBHJIH."

"Do you have a brother or sister, and if so, what is his or her name?"

Aislinn's response: "3FE65."

"What are you holding in your hand right now?"

"I am 14."

And so it continued for all 18 questions. To the amazement of most onlookers in the courtroom, all of Aislinn's answers were utter nonsense. For unclear reasons, even after this remarkable demonstration of the abject failure of FC, the judge still refused to reduce Julian Wendrow's bail. Soon, however, the prosecutors themselves began to harbor serious doubts about the charges against Julian Wendrow. On February 22, 2008, nearly four months after the initial accusation, Julian was released from jail, and on March 10 the prosecutors dropped their case against him. A day later, the Wendrows were reunited with their children. In February 2011, in a landmark settlement against the police, the Wendrows were awarded $1.8 million in damages for the suffering and emotional pain they endured. Acknowledging that the police would reevaluate their procedures in this case, the attorney for the police department, William Hampton, said, "I can't think of anything they [the police] would do differently because we really don't think they did anything wrong."[42]

A number of other facilitated abuse cases against parents, including those of Mark and Laura Storch and the Wheatons, followed parallel plot lines and ended similarly. Although the accused parents were eventually reunited with their children, their lives were torn apart and their reputations badly tarnished. In the 1990s several of these cases garnered considerable media publicity, further fueling doubts regarding the science and ethics of facilitated communication. In this respect, it is remarkable—and troubling—that FC resurfaced in the Wendrow case a decade later. The lessons of these earlier cases had apparently not been learned.

Where had the child abuse allegations originated, and what underlying beliefs in the minds of facilitators led them to plant these often horrific allegations without realizing they were doing so? We may never know for certain. Nevertheless, as we noted earlier, the "abuse narrative" is pervasive in much of popular psychology, and many facilitators may have assumed that children who appeared physically normal—and often seemed to develop typically in their first year—must have experienced a horrific trauma early in life to end up so cognitively impaired. Moreover, the psychogenic views of Bettelheim and other psychoanalytically inclined autism scholars, although debunked by the scientific community, still live on in much of popular culture. What communication researcher Howard Shane terms the *savior effect* may also play a role. Almost all facilitators appear to be caring and well-meaning individuals, and they may feel an obligation to rescue children from what they believe to be a life of grossly inadequate parental treatment, including what they may imagine to be hidden neglect and abuse. Still another source may be misleading information: According to some sources, facilitators in workshops learned that 13% or more of children with autism have been sexually abused.[43] Whatever the reasons, the spate of uncorroborated abuse claims generated by FC seriously damaged the technique's credibility.

By the mid-1990s, the scientific verdict against FC was overwhelming. Scores of major professional organizations, including the American Psychiatric Association, American Psychological Association, Society of the American Academy of Child and Adolescent Psychiatry, American Association on Mental Retardation, and American Academy of Pediatrics, had all issued official policy statements declaring FC ineffective, or at best highly controversial scientifically. In late 1993 the PBS show *Frontline* aired a now-classic exposé on FC entitled *The Prisoners of Silence*, produced by Jon Palfreman.[44] This program and similar exposés by CBS's *60 Minutes* and ABC's *20-20* (both in 1994) further turned the public and professional tide against FC. Although Douglas Biklen continued to operate his Facilitated Communication Institute at Syracuse University, few autism experts outside of the FC community took his claims seriously. Systematic survey data are not available, but it seems clear that the use of FC in school districts around the country plummeted. Still, it continued to be used in some quarters, even as it was dismissed as pseudo-scientific by virtually all autism scholars.

By 2000 FC appeared to be moribund, if not dead. A 2001 published review by psychologist Mark Mostert of Old Dominion University, which reviewed the published research evidence on FC that had accumulated over the previous six years, offered scant more reason for hope. Although acknowledging that a few methodologically flawed studies had yielded supportive or mixed findings, Mostert concluded that studies that had implemented rigorous "control procedures find very little to no support for the efficacy of FC."[45] In a 2005 article titled "The Rise and Fall of Facilitated Communication," Bernard Rimland, a prominent autism researcher, chronicled FC's remarkable ascent and spectacular crash.[46]

Yet, as the philosopher George Santayana wrote famously in 1905, "Those who cannot remember the past are condemned to repeat it." Few had anticipated that popular belief in facilitated communication was about to experience a major comeback. But maybe we shouldn't have been surprised; after all, Clever Hans was succeeded by the supposedly brilliant horses of Elberfeld in Belgium and Beautiful Jim Key and Lady Wonder in the United States.

The Resurgence

We learned from the story of Clever Hans that ideas, unlike people and horses, don't have to die. The self-deception of FC also survived because the general public has a short memory. Moreover, people had never heard of FC in the first place, and others hadn't yet been born when the FC scandal was in the news. A new generation had to learn about the phenomenon we might call the

"Clever Hans effect." What's more, despite substantial scientific progress in our understanding of autism, the condition remained incurable and to a great extent difficult to treat. Even the most effective treatments, including ABA, were far from panaceas. Parents and teachers continued to wish and hope for a discovery that would enable them to "get through to" children with autism. For all these reasons, the stage was set for a surprising resurgence of yet another incarnation of the horse that wouldn't go away.

FIGURE 2.1 POPULAR MEDIA CITATIONS OF FACILITATED COMMUNICATION FROM 1991 TO 2005

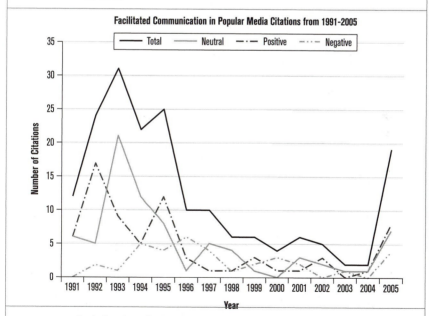

Graph of popular media citations of facilitated communication from 1991 to 2005

Data from Wick, J. and Smith, T. (2009) "Controversial Treatments for Children with Autism in the Popular Media." *ABA Special Interest Group Newsletter,* 25(1), 5-11.

The graphs in Figure 2.1, constructed by psychologists Jennifer Wick and Tristram Smith, tell an intriguing story. As would be expected, the number of mentions of FC in the popular media peaked in the early 1990s, soon after the technique was introduced in the United States and skyrocketed in popularity. Then, also not surprisingly, media coverage declined in the mid- to late 1990s, following the scientific discrediting of the procedure, reaching a nadir for several years beginning at the turn of the 21st century.

Yet something began to change in 2004. It's not entirely clear what happened, but at least some of the sudden surge in media coverage probably stems from the release that year of a beautifully produced documentary, *Autism Is a World*, which was nominated for an Academy Award for Best Documentary Short Subject. *Autism Is a World*, narrated by award-winning actor Julianna Margulies, tells the moving life story of Sue Rubin, a 26-year-old woman who had been diagnosed in childhood with autism. Following IQ testing, she was also diagnosed as mentally retarded and regarded as having the mental age of a 2-year-old, even as a young teenager. At age 13, however, Rubin was introduced to FC, and it forever changed her life. She graduated with a degree in Latin American History from Whittier College in California and became a prominent activist for the rights of people with disabilities to communicate. *Autism Is a World* presented Rubin's voyage of self-discovery, and offered no explicit criticism of FC and no mention of formal independent testing of its claims. The Cable News Network (CNN), which coproduced the film, added to the publicity surrounding the documentary, granting it repeated airtime in May 2005.

Although Figure 2.1 ends abruptly at 2005, the years following 2005 have witnessed a remarkable comeback for FC, strongly suggesting that the line at the end of the graph would continue to surge upward if such a figure were updated today. Oddly, the negative reputation of the technique in the scientific community has not changed at all, nor has any new compelling scientific evidence emerged in support of the procedure. Yet several developments over the past decade or so have conspired to make FC more credible in the eyes of the general public and many practitioners.

In 2005, despite the scientific community's large-scale debunking of FC more than a decade earlier, Douglas Biklen was appointed dean of the School of Education at Syracuse University (a position he held until early 2014), a seeming vindication of his scientific contributions to the developmental disabilities community. Biklen was appointed to this position by Syracuse University President Nancy Cantor, a famous psychologist in her own right and the mother of a child with autism. Meanwhile, FC's use in the schools and communities appeared to expand. A 2006 survey by University of Texas at Austin educational psychologist Vanessa Green and her colleagues[47] revealed that 9.8% of parents of autistic children reported that their children were currently receiving FC, almost certainly a marked increase compared with its use a decade earlier (although systematic survey data from the 1990s are unavailable).

There were still other encouraging developments for advocates of facilitated communication. In 2010 another documentary, *Wretches and Jabberers*, featuring the emotional journey of two men with autism who learned to communicate through FC, opened in more than 100 theaters across the United States.

Although noting that "the film is maddeningly vague about how the two men made their initial breakthroughs," *New York Times* film critic Neil Genzlinger wrote that "it certainly is proof that even those who are written off as children can find a voice."[48] In July 2011 the Media Lab of Massachusetts Institute of Technology, one of the world's premier universities, sponsored a conference on FC with the assistance of Biklen's Syracuse University team.

Douglas Biklen has continued to cement his reputation as a champion of children with disabilities, particularly for his advocacy of expanding communication methods to children presumed to be intellectually impaired. In 2012 he received the United Nations Educational, Scientific and Cultural Organization (UNESCO) Emir Jaber al-Ahmed al-Jaber al-Sabah Prize for his international efforts to enhance communication among individuals with disabilities. In response to the announcement of this prestigious award, Syracuse University President Nancy Cantor stated that "UNESCO's recognition of Doug Biklen's international leadership in scholarship and advocacy for persons with educational disabilities is so well deserved."[49]

Positive media coverage of FC has rebounded, too. In January 2012 the widely read *Huffington Post* featured an uncritical story about Jacob Artson, a nonverbal 17-year-old Los Angeles boy diagnosed with autism and intellectual disability. Informing readers that "a miracle happened" when Jacob discovered FC shortly before his seventh birthday, the article went on to describe his astonishing transformation:

> Perhaps what is most remarkable about Jacob's ability to express himself through typing is how eloquent, thoughtful and intelligent he is. He sent an email to HuffPost

explaining what it was like for him before he could communicate. "Before I was introduced to typing, I had retreated into anxiety, fear and despair. I read everything around me from books to TV credits to the newspaper on the kitchen table but I had no one to share my ideas with so I just retreated into my own imaginary world. I wasn't suicidal because I have an incredibly supportive family, but I was constantly frustrated at my limitations.[50]

In yet another indication of the surprising persistence of facilitated communication in the media, in 2009, numerous major news organizations, including CNN, Fox News, and MSNBC, carried without any hint of skepticism the remarkable feel-good story of Rom Houben. Houben was a 46-year-old Belgian man who had remained in a vegetative state for 23 years following a serious car accident. Although Houben had been presumed for over two decades to be seriously brain-damaged, he suddenly began to type coherent sentences with the help of assistants who steadied his hand. "I shall never forget the day when they discovered what was truly wrong with me. It was my second birth. I want to read, talk with my friends via the computer and enjoy my life now that people know I am not dead."[51] In an online story picked up by multiple news sites, Sky News reported that "an engineering student thought to be in a coma for 23 years was actually conscious the whole time, it has emerged."[52]

Initially, Houben's neurologist Stephen Laureys refused all requests for the independent testing of Houben by outsiders, asserting that he had already verified the authenticity of Houben's communicative abilities. Eventually, after considerable resistance, Houben was administered a message passing test using a new facilitator. A researcher showed him 15 objects with the facilitator out of sight, and then asked him to type their names after the facilitator returned. Houbens failed all 15 trials. Yet these negative results received only minimal media coverage.[53]

To a large extent, FC has succeeded by rebranding itself. Many advocates of the technique no longer use the term, perhaps largely in light of the marked negative connotation it has acquired. Instead, the method is now officially called *supported typing.* A closely related technique, in which an aide moves a letter board slightly in response to the individual's hand motions, is termed **rapid prompting.** Yet rapid prompting is every bit as susceptible to the ideomotor effect as is traditional FC. Douglas Biklen's center at Syracuse University continues to operate and thrive, but under a different name: It is now called the Institute for Communication and Inclusion rather than the Facilitated Communication Institute.

Moreover, many proponents of FC have become more assertive, and perhaps more effective, in their counterattacks against scientific skeptics.[54] In a published article in 2011, one defender of the method even decried scholarly criticisms of FC as "hate speech," contending that "continued anti-FC expression functions as hate speech when it calls into question, without substantiation, the intellectual competence of FC users, thereby undermining their opportunity to exercise their right to freedom of expression."[55] This argument neglects the crucial fact that constructive criticism is the lifeblood of science. Without it, growth in knowledge grinds to a halt. In science, no assertions are immune from critique, as such scrutiny is the very engine of the self-correction that is essential to the scientific endeavor.

We would like to let this chapter conclude with the words of Janyce Boynton, the facilitator in the 1992 Betsy Wheaton sexual abuse case. Janyce Boynton was, in her own words, "a believer and defiant defender" of FC. So, when the evidence did not support what she believed about FC, she faced the same dilemma that Wilhelm von Osten and C. G. Schillings had faced almost 100 years earlier: What will you do when the scientific evidence does not support what you want to believe? Janyce Boynton came to regret her previous role as a facilitator and, like Schillings in the Clever Hans story, became the rare example of someone who can not only admit mistakes but also help others avoid making them. In this respect, she is a role model for the humility that is enforced by living with a scientific attitude. In a 2012 article, she humbly and courageously acknowledged her errors two decades earlier, and offered pointed advice. It is aimed at people who believe in FC, but it is advice that we could all take to heart:

> Find a way to put aside the hurt and shame and speak out about your experience. We cannot erase the damage we have caused by our actions, but we can take responsibility for our part in perpetuating the myth of FC. It is time to put a stop to this practice that adversely affects the very people we set out to protect.[56]

© epa European Pressphoto Agency b.v./Alamy

The Clever Hans Effect in Everyday Life

For lovers of truth, it must always remain a matter of inconsequence whether anyone is pleased or displeased with the truth.

Carl Stumpf

In this brief closing chapter, we'll point out different ways that the Clever Hans effect—our tendency to perceive what we want to believe—infects our everyday thinking. Sometimes the consequences are humorous, at other times embarrassing, and occasionally expensive. But it is always the result of sloppy thinking. The Clever Hans effect can also have profound real-world implications. For example, it can affect our daily behavior by leading us to act in ways that are not helpful, or even harmful, as when Susan taped her windows to protect against the winds of an approaching hurricane. The Clever Hans effect can even influence public policy when we keep paying for expensive, ineffective social programs just because we want to believe in them.[1]

We will also point out ways to resist the Clever Hans effect by developing the skills of clear thinking, objective analysis, and healthy skepticism. However, it is important not to confuse the habit of **healthy skepticism,** which requires open-mindedness to new ideas, with cynicism, which involves close-mindedness. Being too eager to dismiss any claim or belief can be just as detrimental as being too open-minded.[2]

But there's something positive that we can learn from the troubling stories of Clever Hans and facilitated communication. There's an inspiring kind of beauty in learning how to think clearly; it affords us an almost prophetic glimpse into the wonders waiting patiently for future generations who will dare to think scientifically. For example, Charles Darwin's autobiography (written in 1887) records how he felt when a new piece of evidence for that world-changing idea—natural selection—finally took shape in his mind: "I can remember the very spot in the road, whilst in my carriage," Darwin wrote, "when to my joy the solution occurred to me. . . ."[3] It was a wildly creative moment in human understanding when Darwin had what Daniel Dennett describes as "the single best idea anyone has ever had."[4] His habits of thought had produced, during that slender moment, an insight that has helped scientists create life-saving antibiotics, profound advances in understanding our world, and a breathtaking glimpse into a world filled with "endless forms most beautiful and most wonderful."[5] Our belief in positive human potential is why we believe in clear thinking.

But enough inspiration; let's visit Potato.

Potato is a Samoyed dog who belongs to a man named Lu Zesheng in China's Jiangsu province. More particularly, Potato is famous on YouTube as the Chinese math-genius dog. He will correctly bark eight times, for example, when asked how many digits are in 10 million. That may seem like an amazing achievement for a dog, but you don't have to look very hard at the YouTube videos of Potato's performance to witness a likely Clever Hans effect. As Potato barks the final digit of the correct answer, his owner, Lu Zesheng, sharply lifts his chin, a probable cue for Potato to stop. It is fairly safe to conclude that Potato, although adorable, is not a virtuoso of numbers. Still, this did not stop breathless reporting by the world media. For example, the U.K. news source *The Telegraph* informs us that, "According to Chinese state television, Potato can also memorise mobile phone numbers and even people's ages."[6] It's a shame we didn't have YouTube when Clever Hans was busy pawing the ground, but we do have barking Potato.

Another Clever Hans effect is at work among elephants that appear to be painting beautiful landscapes, flowers, images of other elephants, and even self-portraits (search online for elephant painting). If seeing is believing, then these elephants are accomplished artists. But before you surrender a generous amount of money for one of these paintings, you might want to observe closely the people who are handling these elephants. The handlers have learned how to move their hands inside an elephant's ear to direct how the elephant moves the paint brush gripped with the tip of its trunk. It's quite impressive even without the deception that the elephants are doing the actual painting. Each handler learns to direct their elephant to paint just one scene. The thing is . . . isn't it a lot more fun to believe that elephants choose to paint? Well, that probably depends on how much money you paid for your elephant painting. Deceiving ourselves about a counting Chinese dog or a painting elephant is not the worst thing that could happen to us. Some self-deceptions, however, have far more serious consequences.

Drug-Sniffing Labs (or Shepherds or Beagles)

Dogs of many breeds are clever enough to notice cues from people, particularly if they receive rewards for behaving in response to such cues. One of the book's authors (Susan), for example, taught her dog to "read." With regular training and dog treat rewards, the dog learned to move his head slowly back and forth when a book was held in front of him. This innate ability to learn to respond to cues from humans, with whom they coevolved over tens of thousands of years, makes dogs one of the best working animals. Dogs corral sheep, guard businesses after dark, and guide people with visual disabilities. It's also long been thought that dogs' exceptional sense of smell makes them ideal for another job—identifying hidden drugs or hidden bombs.

You may have seen drug-sniffing or bomb-sniffing dogs if you've been in a terminal of a large airport, attended a major sporting event, or visited a famous monument. With their handlers by their side, these dogs have been praised for their uncanny ability to point law enforcement personnel to contraband and the criminals transporting it—and can presumably do so free of the biases that we humans have. A dog, after all, is unlikely to identify suspicious luggage or packages by profiling people based on race, age, gender, attire, or the many other variables that might affect our first impressions.

Moreover, the occasional stories of heroic dogs are vivid and memorable. In 2010 Marine Bradley O'Keefe was injured in Afghanistan by an improvised explosive device (IED) planted by insurgents.[7] O'Keefe credits Earl, his bomb-sniffing Labrador retriever, with saving his life. As the Marine Company approached a foot bridge, O'Keefe explained that Earl "was doing what he does, this thing with his tail," an alert to the Marines that there was an IED in the vicinity. Insurgents blew it up, but because of Earl's alert, the Marines had stopped advancing before the bridge. There were several severe injuries, but no fatalities. O'Keefe returned to the United States for medical treatment, and Earl, after recovering from minor injuries, continued to sniff for bombs. Earl worked with the Marines for a while, then was transferred back to the United States, to the Rhode Island State Police. In that role, among many other assignments, he sniffed for bombs at the finish line in the aftermath of the Boston Marathon bombings. In 2013, after a long search by O'Keefe and his family, O'Keefe and Earl were reunited, and Earl will live out his life as a companion animal. "He slept in the bed with me last night," O'Keefe told reporters. "We are going to spend as much time together as we can."[8]

Despite heartwarming stories like that of Earl and the commonsense feeling that such easily trained animals could excel at sniffing out crime, there is reason to believe that at least some drug- and bomb-sniffing dogs might be yet another version of Clever Hans. For example, Charles Mesloh and his colleagues cautioned, in a review of the literature on scent detection, that research should "require more autonomy on the part of the dog, and off-lead exercises without the handler present may provide greater accuracy of the actual ability of each dog."[9] Without explicitly citing a Clever Hans effect, these authors observed that scent detection had not yet been carefully examined in the absence of the potential for human cues.

Mesloh and colleagues' concerns about the extent of dogs' abilities independent of their handlers are backed by data on dogs' success, or rather lack of success. A governmental study in Australia found a high rate of **false positives** (false identifications); only 26% of over 10,000 alerts led to the discovery of drugs.[10] In another study, the *Chicago Tribune* analyzed three years of police department data on the use of drug-sniffing dogs to provide probable cause for searches of automobiles, and found that only 44% of dogs' alerts led to drugs or drug paraphernalia.[11] Among drivers who were Hispanic, only 27% of searches led to contraband, a possible indication of racial profiling, according to the newspaper article. The *Chicago Tribune* reported that dog handlers argued that the dogs may have been detecting the scent of drugs that had previously been in the car. Nevertheless, the reporters also noted that people who both advocate for and are concerned about the use of drug-sniffing dogs worry that handlers may sometimes cue the dogs, for example, by spending a lot of time examining a particular car.

This circumstantial evidence was bolstered by a carefully designed experiment. Lisa Lit and her colleagues[12] studied 18 pairs of "scent detection dogs" and their handlers, asking the handlers to indicate places where their dog alerted them to scents. In some conditions of the experiment, the researchers told the handlers that there were scents their dogs should be able to pick up, and that visual markers indicated the location of those scents. In reality, neither bomb scents nor drug scents were present, and the study took place in a church that had not been used for scent detection. It was very unlikely that any drugs or bombs had ever been at this site. Therefore, any alert by a dog was almost certainly false.

Nevertheless, handlers frequently reported that their dogs alerted them to one or more scents. Indeed, of 144 searches, only 21 led to no alerts. Lit and her colleagues concluded that two possible explanations existed for these disconcerting find-ings: "Either (1) handlers were erroneously calling alerts on lo-cations at which they believed target scent was located or (2) handler belief that scent was present affected their dogs' alert-ing behavior so that dogs were alerting at locations indicated by handlers (that is, the Clever Hans effect)."[13] Indeed, of the 18 pairs, three handlers were observed to cue their dogs in obvious ways to the supposed presence of a scent. It is not far-fetched to imagine that the other handlers may also have been cuing their dogs, albeit in more subtle—and even unconscious—ways.

Think back to the opening story about Bert and Ernie and the alligators. When we notice only the drug arrests that resulted from an alert from a drug-sniffing dog, we are looking at only one of the possibilities, just as Ernie was paying attention only to the square in which he had a banana in his ear and no alliga-tors were present. The news media tend not to hear about the false positives, the cases in which a dog alerted the handler to drugs or bombs but none were present. And *no one* but the per-son carrying drugs or a bomb knows about the cases in which a drug or bomb is present and a dog does *not* alert a handler. Finally, no one even cares about cases in which innocent people are not detected by dogs.

	DRUGS OR BOMB PRESENT	DRUGS OR BOMB NOT PRESENT
DOG ALERTS HANDLER TO SCENT	Correct alert; these are the ones we pay attention to.	False positives; we never hear about these.
DOG DOES NOT ALERT HANLDER TO SCENT	False negative; no one ever knows about these.	Correct non-alert; we never even think about these.

More research needs to be conducted. Lit and her colleagues, for example, only studied the two boxes in which no contraband was present. It would be helpful to find out if dogs could locate drugs when the handler was told nothing, or was told that no drugs were present. But there's suggestive evidence for a Clever Hans effect in scent detection dogs, at least some of the time. As a society, we should carefully think about whether drug-sniffing dogs are circumventing the need for probable cause in searches, and allowing dog handlers to determine when to conduct a search, whether consciously or not.

It's not just about horses and dogs, of course. Some well-known social interventions also appear to be nothing more than the Clever Hans effect. Here are a few examples, each of which imparts important cautionary lessons about the horse that won't go away.

Scared Straight

Scared Straight (SS) is one of several well-intentioned social programs that have been implemented nationally in recent decades. At first blush, it sounds promising, as FC surely did to many of its advocates. SS identifies teenagers who are considered at risk for delinquency and brings them to an adult prison to hear the stories of prisoners, receive a tour of the facilities, and in some cases spend a day in the prison alongside adult inmates. During SS programs, inmates scream at the young people with the aim of frightening them. As its name suggests, SS provides young people with a terrifying experience that is intended to reduce the likelihood that they will commit crimes in the future.[14]

The program made intuitive sense to policy makers, criminal justice professionals, and worried parents. And scores of young people who had been through the programs tearfully proclaimed that their lives had changed. Despite such moving stories, the evidence *against* SS programs was damning. The best-known review of research on SS found *harmful* effects of SS, with higher rates of future criminal behavior among those who participated in the programs.[15] In one of the more damning studies of SS, 41% of young people who were randomly assigned to attend an SS program committed a new offense within six months. Only 11% of those randomly assigned to a control group committed a new offense during this time frame.[16] In 2007 Lilienfeld listed SS in his article "Psychological Treatments That Cause Harm." The U.S. Department of Justice (DOJ) now refuses to fund SS programs, and points out that SS programs may be violating federal law.[17]

Like the continuing self-deceptions about intelligent horses and FC, the research and DOJ's verdict on SS have not ended these programs. A quick Google search yields details on recent or current programs in locales ranging from Oklahoma to Illinois to Virginia, many of them immortalized in the A&E reality show *Beyond Scared Straight,* first aired in 2011. In the face of ongoing SS programs, a 2011 op-ed by two DOJ officials stated: "The fact that these types of programs are still being touted as effective, despite stark evidence to the contrary, is troubling." Indeed.[18]

Many of these examples of the Clever Hans effect have played on our desire to support things that are good for society: helping people with autism, preventing terror attacks, saving troubled teens from a life of crime, or, in this next case, preventing drug abuse.

The Drug Abuse Resistance Education (D.A.R.E.) Program

The immensely popular Drug Abuse Resistance Education program (D.A.R.E.) is still looking for scientific evidence that it is worth even a fraction of the millions of dollars spent on it each year. Did we say millions? We meant *many* millions. According to Hecht and colleagues,[19] D.A.R.E reaches communities across the United States, in 44 countries, and operates a corporate structure that "is set up like a franchise." But when this book's first author (Tom) first breathed a hint of skepticism about D.A.R.E. to his wife, her immediate reaction was to treat him as if he were some kind of traitor to public virtue. Their children had participated in D.A.R.E. programs and they weren't drug addicts. Isn't that all the proof we need? Tom does not enjoy disagreeing with his wife, but remember Ernie who believed in the protective power of bananas? Ernie was only paying attention to his own experience. Well, the fact that the first author's daughters are not drug addicts is *not* proof that D.A.R.E. is effective.

What about the many careful evaluations into the protective powers of D.A.R.E.? Evaluations indicate that D.A.R.E. is mostly ineffective and may even *promote* mild forms of drug abuse. That's not as ridiculous as it may seem. Populations with high behavioral risk profiles often respond defensively to heavy-handed messages—in other words, the lure of forbidden fruit often becomes stronger for at-risk youth when they are admonished to stay away from it. In addition, the D.A.R.E. program may have communicated the hip language of drug use, making it more familiar and more appealing to teenagers.[20]

How do we know that belief in D.A.R.E. is another self-deceiving expression of the Clever Hans effect? Decades of careful research. Could all that research still be wrong? Of course; that's the scientific way, but D.A.R.E. has been independently evaluated so many times by so many different people that researchers have conducted not just one, but two, meta-analyses—studies of all the studies that gather all the available evidence in one place. D.A.R.E. started at the elementary school level in Los Angeles around 1983 and spread rapidly across the United States. The first meta-analysis was published 10 years later[21] and found only a "slight" and "not statistically significant" influence of D.A.R.E. on reducing drug use even though the researchers evaluated many thousands of participants. Why was D.A.R.E. ineffective? The meta-analysts cited "the relatively low frequency of drug use by the elementary school pupils targeted by DARE's core curriculum."[22] D.A.R.E. was throwing money at a problem that, for the most part, does not exist among these elementary school students.

But what about the delayed effects when these children became teenagers or older? Isn't the real idea behind D.A.R.E. to "get them while they're young," before the problem starts? The 1994 meta-analysis by Ennet and colleagues concluded that "there is no evidence that DARE's effects are activated when subjects are older."[23] The second meta-analysis bluntly concluded that new evidence "supports previous findings indicating that D.A.R.E is ineffective."[24] Since then, the D.A.R.E. program has been revised, but scant evidence exists that the new versions of D.A.R.E., the U.S. version funded by American taxpayers, is doing any better than the original one.[25]

To be fair, one study found a small amount of qualitative evidence that, from a police officer's perspective, D.A.R.E. may help build temporary relationships between officers and youth.[26] But among the many problems with that study is the fact that police departments are on the receiving end of those millions of dollars. That's not much of a justification for three decades of multimillion dollar public investments.[27]

This matters. One of this book's authors had a cousin who died from a drug overdose, and we know that we are not alone in our grief. We desperately want something—anything—to work. Drug abuse often has terrible, far-reaching consequences and the D.A.R.E. program has a wonderful name, nice people, a justification based on education, and a highly visible profile. But unless someone can come up with clear, trustworthy evidence that it is worth all those dollars, the most reasonable conclusion is that D.A.R.E. is nothing more than a multimillion dollar case of spontaneous self-deception; it probably makes its sponsors feel good, but that's about it. Drug abuse is too insidious to waste millions on ineffective programs.

Marketers, of course, have long recognized our willingness to perceive what we already believe. One practical way that clear, critical thinking can save us from ourselves is by saving us money.

Your Baby Can Read

Your Baby Can Read was a series of videos that sold for up to $200, claiming to teach infants to read well before it was thought developmentally possible for most children. Parents could buy the videos at online stores like amazon.com and brick-and-mortar stores including Wal-Mart, Walgreens, Toys "R" Us, and BJ's Wholesale Club. The videos also were marketed directly by Your Baby Can Read, LLC, via a toll-free number advertised through Twitter and Facebook, and through infomercials on a range of channels including YouTube online and the Lifetime, Discovery Kids, and Nickelodeon networks on cable television.[28] The infomercials showed infants viewing words on a screen and then speaking those words out loud.[29] It sure looked as if these babies were reading, and it played very nicely to the familiar mind bug called naive realism, which we've described in the preceding chapters: the very human tendency to assume that we can believe what we see with our own eyes.

Critics pointed out that the infants' "reading" was more likely to be simply memorization of whole words rather than actual reading, and eventually the Federal Trade Commission (FTC) filed false advertising charges against the marketers of *Your Baby Can Read*. The case was settled in the FTC's favor in 2012.[30] In the meantime, however, the company made $185 million from its sales of the product.[31] Why did so many customers fall for the marketing of these videos? Naive realism is once again part of the explanation. The babies in the ads appeared to be reading, and seeing is believing, right? Wrong.

How can we prevent ourselves from falling prey to naive realism? When something seems to be too good to be true—whether it's a horse that can add, a technique that turns children with severe or profound autism into eloquent writers, or a video that teaches babies to read—it probably is too good to be true. We can look beneath the surface by demanding evidence that goes beyond what we can see with our own eyes. Magicians manipulate our perceptions to entertain us—but we know we are being fooled. Companies like Your Baby Can Read manipulate our perceptions to get us to part with our hard-earned money in the belief that what we see is genuine. Once again, we can avoid being fooled if we pay attention to scientific truth tellers who remind us that clear, critical thinking is a virtue that can save us from ourselves.

The chief beneficiaries of clear, critical thinking in this next case are parents who probably have enough to worry about already.

Child Abduction by a Stranger

Are you afraid of shark attacks, dying in an airplane crash, or strangers abducting your children? All these outcomes are extraordinarily unlikely. That is why they are featured in the news, but events that are far more common *and* dangerous are treated as ordinary: deaths from lung cancer, horrific car accidents, and tragic suicides. There is a particular mind bug at work here in which vivid, dramatic events seem to occur far more frequently than they really do. In fact, it is called the *vividness effect* and it leaves us swatting at invisible flies of fear.

For example, many of us know parents who have expressed a fear that their children will be abducted by strangers. Some of us have been those parents—but it wasn't always like this. Historian Paula Fass[32] grouped child abductions into three categories: kidnappings by (1) a family member; (2) a stranger, usually a man, motivated by financial reasons or the intent to abuse the child; and (3) a woman who tries to raise the child as her own. Fass reported: "While the first kind is far and away the most common, it is the second kind of abduction—and the fear it generates—that [has] been most responsible for public hysteria, new public policies, and changes in parental approaches to childrearing."[33] It should also be noted that a third kind of kidnapping—by a woman who attempts to raise the child as her own—is also quite rare and that its victims are typically infants. Most parents worry about kidnapping by a stranger when their preschool or school-age children are playing in the yard or walking to school, and this occurrence is extraordinarily unlikely.[34]

Still, if your child was one of the few abducted in this way, wouldn't you want to know you had done everything possible to prevent this terrible event? What gives us the right to believe that terrified parents are overreacting when they refuse to allow their children to walk to school or play outdoors? A report from the Department of Justice[35] outlined findings from the Second National Incidence Studies of Missing, Abducted, Runaway, and Thrownaway Children (NISMART–2), a report that focused primarily on the year 1999, which the authors viewed as a representative year for such data. In that year, there were 115 cases of what the authors called "stereotypical kidnappings"—the kind that fit what most people think of as stranger abductions. In 1999 approximately 72 million children lived in the U.S.,[36] so the probability of a child being taken by a stranger is 115 out of 72 million, or .00000159.

There are more than 250,000 reported cases of kidnapping by family members per year, so the probability of being part of a *reported* case of kidnapping (even if it turned out to be a false alarm or a misunderstanding related to a custody battle or another issue) was 250,000 out of 72 million, or .000347. This is probably an overestimate because of the false alarm factor. Of those 115 missing children, only 49 of them were killed or never found; the remaining children, 57% of the 115 children who were kidnapped, were returned alive. Certainly this is a tragedy beyond words for the families involved, but it is important to recognize that the chance of this happening in a given year is just 49 out of 72 million, or a probability of .000000681.

What vicious kind of mind bug leads us to fear so intensely something with such a low probability of occurrence? In a survey of parents, Stickler and fellow researchers[37] found that 72% worried that their children would be abducted—about the same as the 75% of parents who worried that their children would be injured in a car accident, and much higher than the 50% of parents who worried about cancer. Fass explored why stranger kidnapping "has come to represent 'a parent's worst nightmare' and why the alarm is so disproportionate to the actual prevalence of the crime."[38] For example, both car accidents and cancer are far more likely to occur than a kidnapping. Indeed, when we look at the data, we see that the top causes of children's death from nonnatural causes are, in order of likelihood: motor vehicle accident; firearm (homicide, suicide, or accident); drowning; fire/burns; poisoning; and suffocation/ strangulation.[39] In 2009 over 9,000 children ages 19 and under died from unintentional injuries—that is, accidents. More specifically, as seen in Figure 3.1, in 2009, 4,564 American children died in car accidents; 1,160 from accidents involving suffocation; 983 from drowning; 824 from poisoning; and 391 from injuries related to a fire or to being burned.[40] Second only to accidents as a cause of death among children, and first among natural causes, is cancer. In 1999 approximately 2,500 children died of cancer.[41]

Our elevated fear of stranger abduction occurs for several reasons. First, the media tend to spotlight the cases that occur. They also engage in fear-mongering with news stories that cite misleading data to exaggerate the likelihood of a child falling victim to a stranger kidnapping. For example, Fass observed that news outlets and victim's groups tend to report combined numbers for *all* missing children, whether they had been kidnapped by strangers, had been abducted by family members, or had wandered or purposely run away from home. The good intentions of these organizations—a desire to raise awareness in the hopes of finding kidnapped children—fuel an unintended public hysteria.

Fass wrote, "At various points in the 1980s, Americans were led to believe that as many as a million children a year were missing and presumed to be the subjects of stranger abductions."[42] Indeed, as of 2013, the Web site parents.com stated that "in 2001, 840,279 people (adults and children) were reported missing to the FBI's National Crime Information Center (NCIC). The FBI estimates that 85 to 90% of those (roughly 750,000 people or 2,000 per day) reported missing were children."[43] Only further down the page does the online article mention that "only about one child out of each 10,000 missing children reported to the local police is not found alive,"[44] and it

FIGURE 3.1   ANNUAL INCIDENCES OF NON-NATURAL CAUSES OF CHILDHOOD DEATHS (AS WELL AS STRANGER KIDNAPPINGS, WHETHER OR NOT THEY RESULTED IN DEATH)

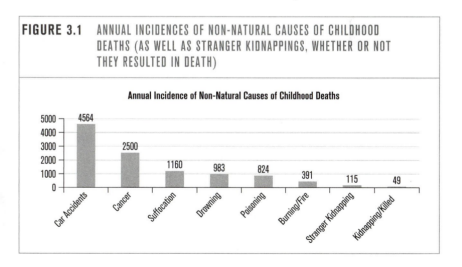

never mentions that the vast majority of these missing children were not abducted by strangers. Furthermore, it never mentions that the vast majority of the children who were not found alive were in the small cohort (115 children out of 72 million) who were abducted by strangers.

As clear, critical thinkers, we can substitute data for mind bugs. For example, the CDC tells us that heart disease is the number one cause of death for people of all ages.[45] Yet most of us don't sit around fearing that every racing of the heart portends death. Shark attacks? If they scare us, we should be far more scared of drowning, or of less evocative, but more deadly, interactions with wildlife: an allergic reaction to a bee sting or a collision between our car and a deer. Airplane crashes? Instead of becoming jittery at the thought of flying, we should be far more worried about driving, as cars are statistically far more lethal than airplanes.

And have you ever worried about psychopaths hiding razor blades in Halloween candy? You're in good company. About 60% of parents in the U.S. share this concern, and many forbid their children to eat candy that is neither well packaged nor from people they know. Yet, one study found *not one single known case* of a stranger hiding a razor blade (or anything else dangerous) in candy, although there was one reported case of a parent doing so.[46] More recent research by sociologist Joel Best uncovered only two incidents, neither of which caused an injury. He concluded, "I have been unable to find a substantiated report of a child being killed or seriously injured by a contaminated treat picked up in the course of trick-or-treating."[47] Best concedes that Halloween is dangerous, but not because of hidden dangers in candy—well, except maybe the excessive sugar. Children are four times as likely to be hit by a car and are much more likely to be injured on Halloween as compared with other nights.[48]

The goal in examining these statistics is not, of course, to make us fear swimming pools, bees, and our cars beyond the caution that all three deserve. Instead, it is to make us place the events that really scare us where they belong—in the realm of events that are far less likely than almost everything we do every single day. This is the case where search engines can be our friend by allowing us to find accurate data to guide our beliefs and actions. An Internet search can lead to reliable data from trustworthy sources. But we need to be critical thinkers when we evaluate the sources of those data because Clever Hans and FC both teach us that expert opinion can be dangerously misleading. The more we actively seek reliable data, the more our fears are in line with the likelihood of potentially dangerous circumstances.

A number of mind bugs feed on the threatening possibility of child abduction by a stranger, starting with the vividness effect and its older cousin, *mental availability* (also called the *availability heuristic*). These misconceptions persist in our thinking because they are often useful, enabling us to make decisions much faster than we would if we had to stop and consider every possible outcome for every possible action. But when a mental shortcut sends our thinking off on a detour, it can take us far from reality. If certain events—like child abductions—come easily to mind, then we are more likely to remember them and worry. So, the kidnappings that make the news increase our fear, and the absence of news about children killed in car accidents lulls us into complacency regarding this far more serious threat. Moreover, if some terrible thing appears to be occurring more commonly, then we are ripe for perceiving an illusory correlation. The end of the story is that loving parents should find something better to worry about, such as driving more carefully—something over which they have far more control.

Sometimes the Clever Hans effect produces self-deceptions that are downright amusing.

Momisms

Ken Jennings has brought attention to culture-specific *momisms*—false beliefs that are widely accepted because many of us heard them as children from our mothers or other caregivers.[49] In the United States, for example, we are counseled not to sit too close to the television because it will "ruin your eyes" and not to swim right after we eat because "you'll get a cramp." These admonitions typically come with the warm, fuzzy feeling of the childhood memories we associate them with. Our warm, fuzzy feelings trump our reason, which is why this mental bug is called the *affect heuristic.*

But these known "truths" vary across cultures, often in humorously contradictory ways. As Jennings wrote, "In China, for example, it's widely believed that sitting on a seat recently warmed by someone else's behind can give you hemorrhoids. The Brits, on the other hand, attribute hemorrhoids to sitting on cold surfaces. But sitting on that same cold concrete would lead to a different lecture from a Ukrainian mom: She'd be sure it would make you sterile."[50] On a bus trip through Bosnia, one of us (Susan) was chastised when she cracked the window on an alarmingly hot bus without air conditioning. Did she want everyone on the bus to catch cold? When we hear a momism from another culture, like the Bosnian fear of drafts, we roll our eyes; but when we are confronted about our own momisms, we typically become defensive. For example, as Americans, how dare you tell us that we can swim immediately after eating?

And yet, it turns out that there is no good reason to wait an hour after eating before going swimming. The Web site snopes. com humorously debunks this myth,[51] even acknowledging that the facts may not sway everyone: "As for those kids who will continue to be sidelined for an hour after eating, . . . they can at least take comfort in the knowledge that they're not being raised in Cuba where the parental belief runs to *three* hours" (italics in the original). The Clever Hans effect shows up as small, amusing Momisms as well as large, socially expensive social programs.

The Last Word

For me, it is far better to grasp the Universe as it really is than to persist in delusion, however satisfying and reassuring.[52]

The story of Clever Hans needs to be retold to each generation. The last two times that the story of Clever Hans was explored were in a report from the New York Academy of Sciences by Thomas Sebeok and Robert Rosenthal in 1981, and again in 1984, when Dodge Fernald wrote a historical essay titled "The Hans Legacy." Fernald compared Pfungst's research methods about Clever Hans to those used by Sigmund Freud in the clinical case known as Little Hans. This book continues that tradition by comparing Pfungst's research methods to those used in the bogus intervention known as facilitated communication.

Think about what the two long stories in this book (Clever Hans and FC) have in common with the seven brief stories we shared (the math-genius dog Potato, the painting elephants, drug- and bomb-sniffing dogs, Scared Straight, the D.A.R.E. program, *Your Baby Can Read* videos, and our wildly exaggerated fears of child abduction). They are all based on popular, well-intended, but false beliefs. They are also beliefs that many people—despite the evidence—stubbornly persist in believing. We even know how people will lie to themselves—by distorting the evidence so that we can continue to believe precisely what we want to believe. These stories also tell us that the Clever Hans effect, while sometimes entertaining, also can lead to real social harm such as false accusations of sexual child abuse, millions of dollars wasted on bogus social programs, and useless anxiety. The story of Clever Hans probably needs to be retold several times and in many ways to each generation.

Does the commonness of the Clever Hans effect mean that we humans stand helpless and at the mercy of that cunning creature in the mirror? No. We are more confused than helpless. And we are confused because we have not learned how to think clearly about our wonderful, complicated, mysterious world. We have reason to be optimistic because most of these illustrations of the Clever Hans effect were exposed as cases of spontaneous self-deception by yet another human invention: psychological science. So do not relegate Clever Hans to a mental category of quaint irrelevance; do not dismiss facilitated communication as a problem for parents and educators of people with autism and similar conditions.

Psychological science is still a young science, not even a teenager, really. It is arguably now only 150 years old and was just starting to walk by the time of the Clever Hans affair. Like all humans, psychologists sometimes make foolish mistakes, blunder into self-deceptions, go on decades-long detours, get caught up in petty academic cultures, and fall for the allure of pop psychology. Nevertheless, we remain optimistic about psychological science because connecting Clever Hans to facilitated communication reminds us that we can all learn how to think more clearly. That confused schoolmaster, Wilhelm von Osten, wanted to make a lasting contribution to science. And ironically, by failing, he succeeded. He gave us a vivid reminder of our propensity toward mental errors that lead to self-deception. That is why Clever Hans is the horse that won't go away—and why we don't want him to.

After-the-fact (post-hoc) explanations *feel as if they are obvious but only after we already know the answers.* (Chapter 1, p. 31)

It only seemed obvious that Clever Hans's musical tastes (for old songs) and abilities (perfect pitch) were really Mr. von Osten's abilities after one knows how von Osten was signaling his horse.

Alternative explanations *remind us that an observed effect usually has many possible causes—it is unwise to believe the first explanation that comes to mind.* (Chapter 1, p. 25)

In addition to the visual signal that proved to be the correct explanation, there were alternative explanations for Clever Hans's apparent abilities, such as genuine intelligence, thought transmissions, and acoustical signals. Proponents of facilitated communication neglected to consider the ideomotor effect (see below) as an alternative explanation for the apparent effectiveness of the technique.

Autism (autism spectrum disorder) *is a condition (now known formally as autism spectrum disorder) marked by impairments in two overarching domains: (1) social communication, including a preference for solitary play and disturbances in eye contact, and (2) repetitive/restricted behaviors, including preoccupations with specific objects and repeated odd movements, such as hand flapping.* (Chapter 2, p. 40)

Believing is seeing *describes how making up our minds ahead of time influences our perceptions.* (Chapter 1, p. 17)

If you believed in Clever Hans's abilities, then you were more likely to perceive exceptional intelligence in the way that the horse held his head and sometimes looked directly at individuals who praised him. If you were convinced that facilitated communication was effective, you were more likely to perceive that individuals with autism were typing independently, without the aid of facilitators.

Clear thinking (critical thinking) *requires mental effort to independently evaluate information.* (Introduction, p. 2)

Those who trusted General Zobel's assessment of Clever Hans deceived themselves because they failed to think on their own, consider alternative explanations, or independently evaluate evidence.

Cognitive dissonance *occurs when we experience psychological tension arising from incompatible beliefs.* (Chapter 1, p. 33)

Mr. von Osten experienced cognitive dissonance when he tried to maintain a belief in Clever Hans's intelligence after Mr. Pfungst's experiments demonstrated that the horse's mathematical abilities vanished when blinders limited his vision.

Confirmation bias *describes our tendency to perceive only evidence that supports what we already believe and to ignore or discount evidence that does not correspond to our beliefs.* (Chapter 1, p. 11)

After the blinders experiment demonstrated that Clever Hans was being signaled, Mr. von Osten refused to let Pfungst and Stumpf conduct any more experiments because, as he wrote in a note, the only purpose of the experiments had been to "corroborate" what Mr. von Osten already believed. Proponents of facilitated communication frequently sought out any evidence that seemed to support the technique, such as a few scattered case reports of successful communication, and neglected or rejected overwhelming evidence from controlled studies indicating that facilitated communication was ineffective.

Developmental dyspraxia *is a supposed motor abnormality that is presumed by some people to prevent individuals with autism from typing independently. This abnormality, which has not been empirically substantiated, justifies the need for a facilitator to steady the individual's hand and arm movements.* (Chapter 2, p. 57)

Extrasensory perception (ESP), *that is, perception occurring outside of the established senses, was one possible explanation for Clever Hans's abilities.* (Chapter 1, p. 17)

Mr. von Osten disappointed believers in ESP because he insisted that Clever Hans was an intelligent horse and that other animals could be trained using similar techniques.

Facilitated communication (FC) *is an unsupported communication intervention on behalf of people without speech; a trained facilitator supposedly can steady the intended movements of people as their fingers hover over an alphabet board or keyboard.* (Chapter 2, p. 41)

FC does not enable people with autism and other disabilities to communicate for themselves; the communications are coming from the facilitator who is unaware that she or he is doing the communicating.

False positives and **false negatives** *occur when you are given inaccurate information, such as a positive pregnancy test even though you are not pregnant (a false positive) or a negative pregnancy test when you really are pregnant (a false negative).* (Chapter 3, p. 92)

The early information about Clever Hans and FC was chock full of false positives; for example, Clever Hans could not add fractions or calculate square roots.

Falsification principle *was articulated by philosopher Sir Karl Popper and proposed that a theory cannot be proven to be true but it can be demonstrated to be false.* (Chapter 1, p. 17)

Mr. von Osten's demonstrations of Clever Hans's abilities seemed convincing until Oskar Pfungst's experiments demonstrated that they were false. Facilitated communication appeared plausible to many of its users, but it was convincingly refuted by rigorously controlled experiments.

Healthy skepticism *is an open-minded attitude that relies on critical thinking and a reluctance to endorse ideas just because they are popular or seem plausible.* (Chapter 3, p. 88)

Psychologists Carl Stumpf and Oskar Pfungst were skeptical about Clever Hans from the beginning, but they were still willing to suspend their judgment until all alternative explanations had been ruled out. Researchers displayed healthy skepticism when they subjected facilitated communication to experimental tests, which allowed them to determine whether the technique was successful or unsuccessful.

Hindsight bias *is also known as the I-knew-it-all-along bias because it describes our tendency to falsely believe that we could have predicted something ahead of time.* (Introduction, p. 6)

Like post-hoc explanations, hindsight bias leads us to believe that we would not have tricked ourselves into believing in Clever Hans if we had been in Berlin, Germany, during the summer of 1904. In retrospect, many of us might say to ourselves, "I never would have been fooled by facilitated communication," but such "20-20 hindsight" is prone to error.

Ideomotor effect *is a phenomenon whereby our thoughts (ideas) influence our actions without our realizing it.* (Chapter 2, p. 69)

This effect is the mechanism whereby facilitated communication, the Ouija board, dowsing, and numerous other phenomena can deceive even highly intelligent individuals.

Illusory correlation *describes the false perception that two things are statistically associated with each other, usually because they happened at the same time.* (Introduction, p. 2)

Asking Clever Hans a question and then watching him tap his hoof with the appropriate answer appeared to be a correlation between the question and the answer that indicated real understanding—but it was a false perception.

Intuition *refers to a way of knowing about something without knowing how we know it.* (Chapter 1, p. 28)

Professor C. G. Schillings's attitude toward Clever Hans was initially skeptical, but his intuition transformed him into a believer after the horse correctly answered his questions; Schillings allowed the evidence to change his mind once again after he observed the results from Pfungst's experiments.

Method of elimination *is the process of systematically testing alternative explanations in order to discover which explanation fits the evidence.* (Chapter 1, p. 25)

Pfungst also planned to test whether Clever Hans was being sent an acoustic signal, but the series of experiments testing a visual signal were so convincing that Mr. von Osten forbid him from conducting any more experiments.

Mind bugs *are a general term for the many false beliefs that lead us to make systematic mental errors of perception.* (Introduction p. 2)

The confirmation bias may be the parent of smaller mind bugs such as believing is seeing, belief perseverance, the hindsight bias, and illusory correlations; they all contributed to misperceiving that Clever Hans was smart enough to perform complex arithmetic in his head even though he was just a hungry horse, and to misperceiving that facilitated communication was working even though controlled studies demonstrated otherwise.

Naïve realism *assumes that we perceive the world as it really is (also called direct realism), rather than the more psychological view that we react to our internal representation of the world (indirect realism).* (Chapter 1, p. 17)

The story of Clever Hans demonstrates indirect realism because what appeared to be true of Clever Hans (that the horse could solve complex mathematical problems) turned out not to be true. To many of its advocates, facilitated communcation seemed to be effective because facilitators observed the successful typing of individuals with autism "with their own eyes."

Parsimony *describes the goal of scientific explanations that explain a great deal of evidence with an extremely simple theory; a parsimonious person is an extreme bargain hunter because she or he wants to get a lot for a little.* (Chapter 1, p. 22)

Oskar Pfungst arrived at a parsimonious explanation for Clever Hans's apparent abilities when he concluded that they were caused by a simple visual signal rather than mysterious thought transmission or complex layers of cognitive abilities.

Phrenology *is the detection of psychological traits by analyzing head bumps.* (Chapter 1, p. 11)

Phrenology had already been scientifically discredited by the time of the Clever Hans affair, but Mr. von Osten's enthusiasm led him to preserve the skull of the first horse he had trained that had died before he could present him to the world.

Post-hoc explanations *are after-the-fact explanations that only seem obvious after we know what caused a particular effect.* (Chapter 1, p. 31)
After knowing that Clever Hans was being signaled by a visual cue, it was easy to explain that the horse's ability to add fractions was not real. After experimental studies demonstrated that facilitated communication did not work, some of its advocates maintained that individuals with autism had repeatedly failed controlled tests only because they were nervous.

Presentism *is a perceptual bias that can occur when we try to explain past events through the lens of present experience.* (Introduction, p. 6)
Our present knowledge of animal intelligence makes it seem unlikely that we would have believed in Clever Hans if we had been there at the time, but we would not know then what we know today.

Principle of least astonishment (POLA) *is, like parsimony, a way of describing the scientific goal of creating explanations that are as simple as possible—and no simpler.* (Chapter 1, p. 22)

Rapid prompting is *a minor variant of facilitated communication in which facilitators move a keyboard or letterpad as the individual with autism is typing.* (Chapter 2, p. 84)

Refrigerator mothers, *that is, mothers who are extremely cold and un-caring, were once believed by some scholars to be the principal cause of autism.* (Chapter 2, p. 48)
This hypothesis, along with other psychosocial explanations for autism, has since been discredited.

Regression to the mean is *a statistical phenomenon whereby extreme scores tend to become less extreme over time.* (Chapter 2, p. 52)
This can lead observers to be fooled by ineffective interventions, such as facilitated communication. For example, parents may bring their

children with autism to treatment when their symptoms are at their worst; as a consequence, even an ineffective intervention (such as facilitated communication) may appear to have an effect on the children's symptoms.

Ruling out *is a term often used when arriving at a medical or psychological diagnosis that involves systematically discarding possible explanations.* (Chapter 1, p. 24)

Oskar Pfungst systematically ruled out alternative explanations for Clever Hans's apparent abilities until the only explanation left was that the horse was responding to some visual signal.

Shaping by successive approximations (or **shaping**) *describes the gradual process of influencing behavior by rewarding intermediate steps that lead to a behavior.* (Chapter 2, p. 71)

Without meaning to, Mr. von Osten shaped Clever Hans's behavior by first rewarding the horse for lifting his hoof, then lifting it and pawing the ground, then pawing the ground multiple times, and so forth.

Spontaneous self-deception *emphasizes that self-deception can occur without deliberate intention to deceive.* (Chapter 1, p. 23)

The confusion over Clever Hans arose naturally; no one set out to make money or trick others into believing in Clever Hans. Almost certainly, facilitators had persuaded themselves that individuals with autism were doing the typing, and that they played no direct role in this typing,

Telepathy (or **thought transference**) *refers to communication through psychic thought transmission, something that has yet to be demonstrated as possible.* (Chapter 1, p. 24)

Historian Dodge Fernald asserts that Sigmund Freud was interested in the possibility of telepathy in the case of Clever Hans, and encouraged a friend to observe and write about it.

Texas sharpshooter fallacy *is a descriptive name for the hindsight bias that compares after-the-fact explanations to a sharpshooter who first shoots holes in the barn wall and then draws target circles around the holes.* (Chapter 1, p. 32)

Professor C. G. Schillings became a Texas sharpshooter when he pointed out the visual cue of leaning forward and backward—but only after Pfungst's experiments convinced him that the visual cue was responsible for Clever Hans's apparent abilities.

With knowledge and **without knowledge** *describe experimental conditions that can test whether some kind of signal is being sent in cases of apparently remarkable abilities.* (Chapter 1, p. 26)

In the "with knowledge" condition, Mr. von Osten could see a card indicating how many time Clever Hans should tap his hoof; in the "without knowledge" condition, Mr. von Osten could not see the card indicating how many times Clever Hans should tap his hoof.

INTRODUCTION

[1]Fine, C. (2006). *A mind of its own: How your brain distorts and deceives.* New York: W. W. Norton. See also VanLehn, K. (1990). *Mind bugs: The origins of procedural misconceptions.* Cambridge, MA: MIT Press.

[2]National Weather Service. (2005). *Hurricane watch—Inland safety.* Retrieved from http://tinyurl.com/msyx7d3

[3]Lilienfeld, S. O., Lynn, S. J., Namy, L., & Woolf, N. (2013). *Psychology: From inquiry to understanding.* Boston: Allyn & Bacon.

CHAPTER 1

[1]Fernald, D. (1984). *The Hans legacy.* Hillsdale, NJ: Erlbaum. See also Sanford, E. (1914). Psychic research in the animal field: *Der Kluge Hans* and the Elberfeld horses. *American Journal of Psychology, 25,* 1–31.

[2]Pfungst, O. (1911). *Clever Hans (the horse of von Osten).* New York: Henry Holt, p. 13.

[3]Sanford, E. C. (1914). Psychic research in the animal field, *The American Journal of Psychology,* XXV, 1, p. 2.

[4]Fernald, *The Hans legacy: A story of science.* Hillsdale, NJ: Erlbaum, p. 41.

[5]Hochschild, A. (2011). *To end all wars: A story of loyalty and rebellion, 1914–1918.* Boston: Houghton Mifflin Harcourt, pp. 41, 367.

[6]Ibid., p. 142.

[7]Pfungst, *Clever Hans,* p. 38.

[8]Ibid., p. 25.

[9]Schillings, C. G. (1905). *With flashlight and rifle.* New York: Harper & Brothers, p. 47.

[10]Pfungst, *Clever Hans,* p.18.

[11]Ibid., p. 25.

[12]Fernald, *The Hans legacy,* p. 30.

[13]Lilienfeld, S. O., Lynn, S. J., Ruscio, J., & Beyerstein, B. L. (2010). The five great myths of popular psychology: Implications for psychotherapy. In D. David, S. J. Lynn, & A. E. Ellis (Eds.), *Rational and irrational beliefs:*

Research, theory, and practice (pp. 313–338). New York: Oxford University Press.

[14]Pfungst, *Clever Hans*, p. 246.

[15]Ibid., pp. 248–249.

[16]Fernald, *The Hans legacy*, p. 213. See also Jones, E. (1957). *The life and work of Sigmund Freud* (Vol. 3). New York: Basic Books.

[17]Pfungst, *Clever Hans*, p. 71.

[18]Ibid., p. 90.

[19]Ibid.

[20]Ibid.

[21]Ibid., 31.

[22]Ibid., p. 202.

[23]Ibid.

[24]Ibid., p. 60.

[25]Ibid., p. 1.

[26]Ibid., p. 63.

[27]Ibid., p. 91.

[28]Ibid., p. 103.

[29]Ibid., p. 235.

[30]Ibid., p. 24.

[31]Ibid., p. 57.

[32]Ibid., p. 13.

[33]Ibid.

[34]Ibid., p. 228.

[35]Ibid., p. 41.

[36]Maeterlinck, M. (2008/ 1914). *Clever Hans and the Elberfeld horses.* (Equestrian Wisdom and History Series). The Long Riders' Guild Press, p. 32.

[37]Fernald, *The Hans legacy*, p. 198.

[38]Ibid., p. 195.

[39]Zusne, L. (1984). *Biographical dictionary of psychology.* Westport, CT: Greenwood Press.

[40]Maeterlinck, *Clever Hans and the Elberfeld horses.*

[41] Griffith, A. C. (June 14, 2003). *Richmond then and now: Index of Lady Wonder items.* Retrieved from http://richmondthenandnow.com/Lady-Wonder-Index.html

⁴²Gardner. M. (1952). *In the name of science.* Mineola, NY: G. P. Putnam's Sons.

⁴³Kavoor, A. T. (1998). *Begone godmen: Encounters with spiritual frauds.* Mumbai, India: Jacob Publishing House.

CHAPTER 2

¹Kanner, L. (1943). Autistic disturbances of affective contact. *Nervous Child, 2,* 217–250.

²Ibid., p. 218.

³Asperger, H. (1944). Die "autistischen psychopathen" im kindesalter [Autistic psychopathology in childhood]. *European Archives of Psychiatry and Clinical Neuroscience, 117,* 76–136.

⁴American Psychiatric Association. (2013). *Diagnostic and statistical manual of mental disorders* (5th ed.). Washington, DC: Author.

⁵ Kanner, L. (1943). Autistic disturbances of affective contact. *Nervous Child, 2,* p. 217–250.

⁶See Boushéy, A. (2004). *Parent to parent: Information and inspiration for parents dealing with autism or Asperger's syndrome.* London: Kingsley Publishers, p. 35.

⁷Bettelheim, B. (1967). *The empty fortress.* New York: Simon & Schuster.

⁸Hertz-Picciotto, I., Croen, L. A., Hansen, R., Jones, C. R., van de Water, J., & Pessah, I. N. (2006). The CHARGE study: An epidemiologic investigation of genetic and environmental factors contributing to autism. *Environmental Health Perspectives, 114,* 1119–1125.

⁹Dawson, G. (2013). Dramatic increase in autism prevalence parallels explosion of research into its biology and causes. *JAMA Psychiatry, 70,* 9–10.

¹⁰Virués-Ortega, J. (2010). Applied behavior analytic intervention for autism in early childhood: Meta-analysis, meta-regression and dose–response meta-analysis of multiple outcomes. *Clinical Psychology Review, 30,* 387–399.

¹¹Romanczyk R. G., Arnstein, L., Soorya, L., & Gillis, J. (2003). The myriad of controversial treatments for autism: A critical evaluation of efficacy. In Lilienfeld, S. O., Lynn, S. J., & Lohr, J. M. (Eds.), *Science and pseudoscience in clinical psychology* (pp. 363–395). New York: Guilford Press.

¹²Miller, L. K. (1999). The savant syndrome: Intellectual impairment and exceptional skill. *Psychological Bulletin, 125,* 31–46.

[13]Lilienfeld, S. O., Lynn, S. J., Ruscio, J., & Beyerstein, B. L. (2010). The five great myths of popular psychology: Implications for psychotherapy. In D. David, S. J. Lynn, & A. E. Ellis (Eds.), *Rational and irrational beliefs: Research, theory, and practice* (pp. 313–338). New York: Oxford University Press.

[14]Chabris, C., & Simons, D. J. (2010). *The invisible gorilla: And other ways our intuitions deceive us.* New York: Random House.

[15]Patihis, L., Ho, L. Y., Tingen, I. W., Lilienfeld, S. O., & Loftus, E. F. (2013). Are the "memory wars" over? A scientist–practitioner gap in beliefs about repressed memory. *Psychological Science, 25,* 519-530. doi:10.1177/0956797613510718

[16]Lilienfeld, S. O. (2012). Public skepticism of psychology: Why many people perceive the study of human behavior as unscientific. *American Psychologist, 67,* 111–129.

[17]Herbert, J. D., Sharp, I. R., & Gaudiano, B. A. (2002). Separating fact from fiction in the etiology and treatment of autism. *Scientific Review of Mental Health Practice, 1,* 25–40.

[18]Jacobson, J. W., Mulick, J. A., & Schwartz, A. A. (1995). A history of facilitated communication: Science, pseudoscience, and antiscience science working group on facilitated communication. *American Psychologist, 50,* 750–765.

[19]Ibid.

[20]Biklen, D. (1990). Communication unbound: Autism and praxis. *Harvard Educational Review, 60,* 291–315.

[21]Ibid.

[22]Green, G. (1994). Facilitated communication: Mental miracle or sleight of hand? *Skeptic, 2*(3), 68–76.

[23]Kaplan, R. (Producer). (1992, January 25, 1992). *Primetime Live.* New York: ABC. Quoted in Palfreman, J. (Producer). (1993, October 19). Prisoners of silence [Televiseries episode]. *Frontline.* New York: WNET. Retrieved from http:// tinyurl.com/bj52lje.

[24]Palfreman, J. (Producer). (1993, October 19). Prisoners of silence [Televiseries episode]. *Frontline.* New York: WNET. Retrieved from http:// tinyurl.com/bj52lje.

[25]Ibid.

[26] Ibid.

[27]Bedward, Roy. "Please Listen to My Heart." *GLIMPSE*, 2007. Reprinted with permission from ICDL.

[28]Marvin, U. B. (1985). The British reception of Alfred Wegener's continental drift hypothesis. *Earth Sciences History, 4,* 138–159.

[29]Dawes, R. M. (1994). *House of cards: Psychology and psychotherapy built on myth.* New York: Free Press.

[30]Valenstein, E. S. (1986). *Great and desperate cures: The rise and decline of psychosurgery and other radical treatments for mental illness.* New York: Basic Books.

[31]Jacobson, J. W., Mulick, J. A., & Schwartz, A. A. (1995). A history of facilitated communication.

[32]Lilienfeld, S. O. (2005). Scientifically unsupported and supported interventions for childhood psychopathology: A summary. *Pediatrics, 115,* 761–764. See also Mostert, M. (2001). Facilitated communication since 1995: A review of published studies. *Journal of Autism and Developmental Disorders, 31,* 287–313.

[33]Jacobson, J. W., Mulick, J. A., & Schwartz, A. A. (1995). A history of facilitated communication: Science, pseudoscience, and atiscience. (Science Working Group on facilitated communication). *American Psychologist, 50,* 750–765.

[34]Mostert, M. Facilitated communication since 1995.

[35]Meehl, P. E. (1967). Theory-testing in psychology and physics: A methodological paradox. *Philosophy of Science, 34,* 103–115.

[36]Spitz, H. H. (1997). *Nonconscious movements: From mystical messages to facilitated communication.* Mahwah, NJ: Erlbaum.

[37]Hochschild, A. (2011). *To end all wars: A story of loyalty and rebellion, 1914–1918.* Boston: Houghton Mifflin Harcourt, p. 222.

[38]Spitz, *Nonconscious movements.* See also Wegner, D. M. (2002). *The illusion of conscious will.* Cambridge, MA: MIT Press.

[39]Easton, R. D., & Shor, R. E. (1976). An experimental analysis of the Chevreul pendulum illusion. *The Journal of General Psychology, 95,* 111–125.

[40]Wegner, D. M., Fuller, V. A., & Sparrow, B. (2003). Clever hands: Uncontrolled intelligence in facilitated communication. *Journal of Personality and Social Psychology, 85,* 5–19.

[41]Palfreman, J., Prisoners of silence.

[42]Wisely, J., & Brasier, L. L. (2010, December 12). Dad's arrest in sex case results in $1.8 M settlement. Freep.com. Retrieved from http://www.deborahgordonlaw.com/Practice-Areas/Media-Coverage/Dads-arrest-in-sex-case-results-in-1-8M-settlement.shtml

[43]Autism Society. (2014). *Living with autism: Information for child abuse counselors.* Retrieved from http://www.autism-society.org/files/2014/04/Child_Abuse_Counselors.pdf.

[44]Palfreman, J., Prisoners of silence.

[45]Mostert, M. Facilitated communication since 1995.

[46]Rimland, B. (2005). Facilitated communication: Its rise and fall. *Autism Research Institute, 19*(2). Retrieved from http://legacy.autism.com/ari/editorials/ed_risefallfaccomm.htm

[47]Green, V. A., Pituch, K. A., Itchon, J., Choi, A., O'Reilly, M., & Sigafoos, J. (2006). Internet survey of treatments used by parents of children with autism. *Research in Developmental Disabilities, 27*(1), 70–84.

[48]Genzlinger, N. (2011, March 31). Traveling with autism. *New York Times.* Retrieved from http://www.nytimes.com/2011/04/01/movies/wretches-jabberers-a-documentary-on-autism-review.html?_r=0.

[49]Syracuse.com (February 28, 2012). Syracuse University education school dean to be honored in Kuwait. Retrieved from http://www.syracuse.com/news/index.ssf/2012/02/syracuse_university_education.html

[50]Miles, K. (2012). Jacob Arson, LA teen with autism, communicates through typing. *Huffington Post.* Retrieved from http://www.huffingtonpost.com/2012/01/12/jacob-artson-teen-autism-typing_n_1184950.html.

[51]New York Post (2009, November 23). Awake through a 23-year 'coma'. Retrieved from http://nypost.com/2009/11/23/awake-through-a-23-year-coma/

[52]Watts, A. (2009, November 23). Man trapped in 23-year "coma" was conscious. Retrieved from http://news.sky.com/story/740302/man-trapped-in-23-year-coma-was-conscious

[53]Boudry, M., Termote, R., & Betz, W. (2010). Fabricating communication. *Skeptical Inquirer, 34,* 4.

[54]Todd, J. T. (2012). The moral obligation to be empirical: Comments on Boynton's "Facilitated Communication—What harm it can do:

Confessions of a former facilitator." *Evidence-Based Communication Assessment and Intervention, 6,* 36–57.

⁵⁵Stubblefield, A. (2011). Sound and fury: When opposition to facilitated communication functions as hate speech. *Disability Studies Quarterly, 31*(4). Retrieved from http://dsq-sds.org/article/view/1729/1777

⁵⁶Boynton, J. (2012). Facilitated communication—What harm it can do: Confessions of a former facilitator. *Evidence-Based Communication Assessment and Intervention, 6,* 3–13.

CHAPTER 3

¹Lilienfeld, S. O., Ammirati, R., & David, M. (2012, February). Distinguishing science from pseudoscience in school psychology: Science and scientific thinking as safeguards against human error. *Journal of School Psychology, 50*(1), 7–36.

²Lilienfeld, S. O. (2005). The 10 commandments of helping students distinguish science from pseudoscience in psychology. *APS Observer, 18*(9), 39–40.

³Darwin, C. (1887/ 2010). *The autobiography of Charles Darwin.* London: Bibliolis Books, p. 83.

⁴Dennett, D. (1995). *Darwin's dangerous idea.* New York: Simon & Schuster, p. 21.

⁵Darwin, C. (1869). *On the origin of species by means of natural selection* (5th ed.). London: John Murray, p. 579.

⁶Reuters. (2012, December 8). Chinese dog is "math genius," according to owner. *The Telegraph.* Retrieved from http://www.telegraph.co.uk/news/newsvideo/weirdnewsvideo/9731570/Chinese-dog-is-maths-genius-according-to-owner.html.

⁷Retired Marine Brad O'Keefe reunites with Earl, the bomb-sniffing dog that saved his life. (2013, July 1). *Huffington Post.* Retrieved from http://www.huffingtonpost.com/2013/07/01/brad-okeefe-earl_n_3529943.html

⁸Ibid.

⁹Mesloh, C., Wolf, R., & Henych, M. (2002). Scent as forensic evidence and its relationship to the law enforcement canine. *Journal of Forensic Identification, 52*(2), 169–182.

[10]NSW Ombudsman. (2006). *Review of the Police Powers (Drug Detection Dogs) Act 2001.* Retrieved from http://www.ombo.nsw.gov.au/__data/assets/pdf_file/0020/4457/Review-of-the-Police-Powers-Drug-Detection-Dogs-Part-1_October-2006.pdf

[11]Hinkel, D., & Mahr, J. (2011, January 6). *Tribune* analysis: Drug-sniffing dogs in traffic stops often wrong. *Chicago Tribune.* Retrieved from http://articles.chicagotribune.com/2011-01-06/news/ct-met-canine-officers-20110105_1_drug-sniffing-dogs-alex-rothacker-drug-dog

[12]Lit, L., Schweitzer, J. B., & Oberbauer, A. M. (2011). Handler beliefs affect scent detection dog outcomes. *Animal Cognition, 14*(3), 387–394.

[13]Ibid., p. 392.

[14]Robinson, L. O., & J. Slowikowski. (2011, January 31). Scary—and ineffective. *The Baltimore Sun.* Retrieved from http://articles.baltimoresun.com/2011-01-31/news/bs-ed-scared-straight-20110131_1_straight-type-programs-straight-program-youths

[15]Petrosino, A., Turpin-Petrosino, C., & Finckenauer, J. O. (2000). Well-meaning programs can have harmful effects! Lessons from experiments of programs such as Scared Straight. *Crime & Delinquency, 46*(3), 354–379. See also Petrosino, A., Turpin-Petrosino, C., Hollis-Peel, M. E., & Lavenberg, J. G. (2013, April 30). Scared Straight and other juvenile awareness programs for preventing juvenile delinquency. *The Cochrane Library.* Retrieved from http://onlinelibrary.wiley.com/doi/10.1002/14651858.CD002796.pub2/pdf

[16]Finckenauer, J. O. (1982). *Scared straight and the panacea phenomenon.* Englewood Cliffs, NJ: Prentice-Hall.

[17]U.S. Department of Justice. (2011, March/April). Justice Department discourages the use of "Scared Straight" programs. Retrieved from https://www.ncjrs.gov/html/ojjdp/news_at_glance/234084/topstory.html

[18]Robinson, L. O., & J. Slowikowski, Scary—and ineffective.

[19]Hecht, M. L., Colby, M., & Miller-Day, M. (2010). The dissemination of *keepin' it REAL* through D.A.R.E.: A lesson in disseminating health messages. *Health Communications, 25,* 585–586.

[20]Schüz, N., Schüz, B., & Eid, M. (2013). When risk communication backfires: Randomized controlled trial on self-affirmation and reactance to personalized risk feedback in high-risk individuals. *Health Psychology, 32,* 561–570.

[21]Ennett, S. T., Tobler, N. S., Ringwalt, C. L., & Flewelling, R. L. (1994). How effective is drug abuse resistance education? A meta-analysis of Project DARE outcome evaluations. *American Journal of Public Health, 84,* 1394–1401, p. 1398.

[22]Ibid., p. 1399.

[23]Ibid., p. 1399.

[24]West, S. L., & O'Neal, K. K. (2004). Project D.A.R.E. outcome effectiveness revisited. *American Journal of Public Health, 94,* 1027–1029.

[25]Singh, R. D., Jimerson, S. R., Renshaw, T., Saeki, E., Hart, S. R., Earhart, J., & Stewart, K. (2011). A summary and synthesis of contemporary empirical evidence regarding the effects of the Drug Abuse Resistance Education Program (D.A.R.E.). *Contemporary School Psychology, 15,* 93–102.

[26]Hansen, I. (2012). D.A.R.E.: The message and the messenger—Perspectives of the officer. *Dissertation Abstracts International Section A: Humanities and Social Sciences, 72,* 4789.

[27]Birkeland, A., Murphy-Graham, E., & Weiss, C., (2005). Good reasons for ignoring good evaluation: The case of the drug abuse resistance education (D.A.R.E.). *Education and Program Planning, 28,* 247–256.

[28]Federal Trade Commission (FTC). (2012, August 28). Ads touting "Your Baby Can Read" were deceptive, FTC complaint alleges. Retrieved from http://www.ftc.gov/news-events/press-releases/2012/08/ads-touting-your-baby-can-read-were-deceptive-ftc-complaint

[29]Your Baby Can Read infomercial. Retrieved from http://www.youtube.com/watch?v=2qoqs-GeBj0

[30]FTC, Ads touting "Your Baby Can Read."

[31]Ibid.

[32]Fass, P. (2010). Child kidnapping in America. *Origins: Current Events in Historical Perspective, 3.* Retrieved from http://origins.osu.edu/article/child-kidnapping-america

[33]Ibid.

[34]Ibid.

[35]Finkelhor, D., Hammer, H., & Sedlak, A. J. (2002). *Nonfamily abducted children: National estimates and characteristics.* Washington, DC: National Incidence Studies of Missing, Abducted, Runaway, and Throwaway Children, Office of Juvenile Justice and Delinquency Prevention,

U.S. Department of Justice. Retrieved from https://www.ncjrs.gov/html/ojjdp/nismart/03/

[36]Childstats.gov. *POP1: Child population.* (2013) Retrieved from http://www.childstats.gov/americaschildren/tables/pop1.asp

[37]Stickler, G. B., Salter, M., Broughton, D. D., & Alario, A. (1991). Parents' worries about children compared to actual risks. *Clinical Pediatrics, 30*(9), 522–528.

[38]Fass, Child kidnapping in America.

[39]National MCH Center for Child Death Review. *United States: Child mortality, 2010.* (2013) Retrieved from http://www.childdeathreview.org/nationalchildmortalitydata.htm

[40]Centers for Disease Control and Prevention. (2012, April 20). Vital signs: Unintentional injury deaths among persons aged 0–19 years—United States, 2000–2009. *Morbidity and Mortality Weekly Report (MMWR), 61*(15), 270–276. Retrieved from http://www.cdc.gov/mmwr/preview/mmwrhtml/mm6115a5.htm?s_cid=mm6115a5_w

[41]American Childhood Cancer Organization. *Childhood cancer statistics.* (2014) Retrieved from https://www.acco.org/Information/AboutChildhoodCancer/ChildhoodCancerStatistics.aspx

[42]Fass, Child kidnapping in America.

[43]Bilich, K. A. (2014). Child abduction facts. *Parents.com,* Retrieved from http://www.parents.com/kids/safety/stranger-safety/child-abduction-facts/

[44]Ibid.

[45]Hoyert, D. L., & Xu, J. (2012, October 10). Deaths: Preliminary data for 2011. *National Vital Statistics Reports, 61*(6). Retrieved from http://www.cdc.gov/nchs/data/nvsr/nvsr61/nvsr61_06.pdf

[46]Heath, C., & Heath, D. (2007). *Made to stick: Why some ideas survive and others die.* New York: Random House.

[47]Best, J. (2012). *Halloween sadism: The evidence.* Retrieved from http://www.udel.edu/soc/faculty/best/site/halloween.html

[48]Ibid.

[49]Jennings, K. (2013, January 22). Is your electric fan trying to kill you? *Slate.* Retrieved from http://www.slate.com/articles/life/for-

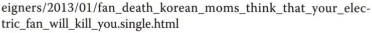

eigners/2013/01/fan_death_korean_moms_think_that_your_electric_fan_will_kill_you.single.html

[50]Ibid.

[51]Snopes.com. Hour Missed Brooks. (April 2012) Retrieved from http://www.snopes.com/oldwives/hourwait.asp

[52]Sagan, C. (1997). *The demon-haunted world: Science as a candle in the dark.* New York: Ballantine Books.